Becoming an Expert Witness in Health Care and Litigation

A Beginner's Guide

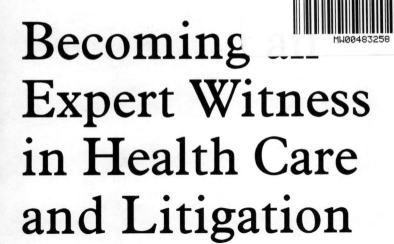

Becoming an Expert Witness in Health Care and Litigation

A Beginner's Guide

Jeff G. Konin, PhD, ATC, PT, FACSM, FNATA

Mark S. Ramey, Esq

SLACK Incorporated
6900 Grove Road
Thorofare, NJ 08086 USA
856-848-1000   Fax: 856-848-6091
www.slackbooks.com
ISBN: 978-1-63091-848-4
© 2023 by SLACK Incorporated

Vice President, Editorial: Jennifer Kilpatrick
Vice President, Marketing: Mary Sasso
Acquisitions Editor: Brien Cummings
Director of Editorial Operations: Jennifer Cahill
Vice President/Creative Director: Thomas Cavallaro
Cover Artist: Katherine Christie

Dr. Jeff G. Konin, Mark S. Ramey *and* Eric F. Quandt *have no financial or proprietary interest in the materials presented herein.*

The procedures and practices described in this publication should be implemented in a manner consistent with the professional standards set for the circumstances that apply in each specific situation. Every effort has been made to confirm the accuracy of the information presented and to correctly relate generally accepted practices. The authors, editors, and publisher cannot accept responsibility for errors or exclusions or for the outcome of the material presented herein. There is no expressed or implied warranty of this book or information imparted by it. Care has been taken to ensure that drug selection and dosages are in accordance with currently accepted/recommended practice. Off-label uses of drugs may be discussed. Due to continuing research, changes in government policy and regulations, and various effects of drug reactions and interactions, it is recommended that the reader carefully review all materials and literature provided for each drug, especially those that are new or not frequently used. Some drugs or devices in this publication have clearance for use in a restricted research setting by the Food and Drug and Administration or FDA. Each professional should determine the FDA status of any drug or device prior to use in their practice.

Any review or mention of specific companies or products is not intended as an endorsement by the author or publisher.

SLACK Incorporated uses a review process to evaluate submitted material. Prior to publication, educators or clinicians provide important feedback on the content that we publish. We welcome feedback on this work.

Library of Congress Control Number: 2022943181

For permission to reprint material in another publication, contact SLACK Incorporated. Authorization to photocopy items for internal, personal, or academic use is granted by SLACK Incorporated provided that the appropriate fee is paid directly to Copyright Clearance Center. Prior to photocopying items, please contact the Copyright Clearance Center at 222 Rosewood Drive, Danvers, MA 01923 USA; phone: 978-750-8400; website: www.copyright.com; email: info@copyright.com

Printed in the United States of America.

Last digit is print number: 10   9   8   7   6   5   4   3   2   1

DEDICATION

To all of the attorneys I have worked with in my career that have taught me all about the legal system, especially Stephen E. Geduldig, who was my first legal mentor and patiently crafted my entry-level expert skills.

—*Jeff G. Konin, PhD, ATC, PT, FACSM, FNATA*

To the little-known hockey team that introduced me to my coauthor and allowed us to play as teammates, and my number one paralegal who was instrumental in completion of this book.

—*Mark S. Ramey, Esq*

CONTENTS

ACKNOWLEDGMENTS

A simple yet heartfelt thank you to all of those whom I have had the pleasure to work with and learn from through my exciting ventures into risk management and the legal aspects of my academic, scientific, administrative, and clinical career.

I would also like to thank my colleagues and friends at SLACK Incorporated: Brien Cummings and Jennifer Cahill and also Rashmi Malhotra at Westchester Publishing Services, the production project manager.

—*Jeff G. Konin, PhD, ATC, PT, FACSM, FNATA*

To the multitude of experts I have had the pleasure to work with and who patiently taught me what I think I know and the many clients who have trusted my skills and abilities, allowing me to represent them over the years.

—*Mark S. Ramey, Esq*

ABOUT THE AUTHORS

Jeff G. Konin, PhD, ATC, PT, FACSM, FNATA, is a Clinical Professor at Florida International University, in Miami, Florida. He has been a leading clinician, educator, and scholar for more than 30 years. As a licensed and certified athletic trainer and licensed physical therapist, Dr. Konin is the author of more than 25 academic textbooks and has delivered hundreds of professional presentations throughout the world. He is a recognized Fellow of the American College of Sports Medicine and the National Athletic Trainers' Association (NATA), and a member of the NATA's Hall of Fame.

Dr. Konin is a Founding Partner of The Rehberg Konin Group, dedicated to providing expert advice in the area of sport safety, education, and other areas. Over the past 20+ years, he served in various expert roles for both the plaintiff and defendant. He has consulted with organizations, businesses, and academic institutions on various matters of risk management and prevention. Dr. Konin is a contributing writer for *Sports Medicine Legal Digest,* and in 2019, he was recognized by the NATA for Distinction in the Advancement of Legal, Ethical and Regulatory Issues.

Mark S. Ramey, Esq, is a practicing trial attorney and founding partner of Ramey & Kampf, P.A. in Tampa, Florida. After receiving his Doctorate of Jurisprudence degree from Stetson University College of Law in 1987, he served as an Assistant State Attorney for the Sixth Judicial Circuit Florida until 1994. While a felony prosecutor, he tried cases ranging from murder to arson to trafficking to racketeering. Since entering private practice, his career has been devoted solely to insurance defense, litigating cases through trial on behalf of major insurance institutions for nearly 30 years. He is admitted to practice in all Florida courts, as well as the U.S. District Court for the Middle District of Florida, the U.S. Court of Appeals for the 11th Circuit, and the U.S. Supreme Court.

PREFACE

When two parties meet and are of differing opinions, it takes a mountain of inquiry to essentially relive the experience to determine which side bears responsibility for an incident. In medicine and health, this typically entails an injured party who claims stake that they were wronged in such a way that a defending party caused such injury. A legal claim initiates the process of inquiry that is spearheaded by attorneys who navigate the complexities of the legal system.

As evidence is gathered from both sides to better understand the cause or causes that led up to the actual injury, oftentimes attorneys will lean toward the opinion of a professional whose expertise aligns with the nature of the injury. These expert witnesses can include medical doctors or any other health care provider, such as nurses, athletic trainers, physical therapists, biomechanists, exercise scientists, and even strength and conditioning specialists.

It is not always an easy task for an attorney to find that perfect expert. Why is it so challenging to do so when there are truly so many good medical and health care providers in our communities? Simply put, the art and science of being an expert witness in the legal system is not the same as being an expert clinician, scientist, or educator. Most of us have watched enough television to think we could take the stand and testify, haven't we? In fact, we probably think we could even be a good lawyer! Well, as the old adage goes, let the lawyer play lawyer and let the expert be an expert. To play this out, the lawyer has been professionally educated, passed a bar exam, and practices the trade every day. By contrast, the expert witness likely has a full-time job practicing medicine or health care of some kind and merely serves as an expert on occasion with no formal training to do so. There are always exceptions. For example, there are bad lawyers, and there are experts who do receive formal training. Nonetheless, being an expert witness in any capacity is not a role for the weary. It can be uncomfortable and stressful, attack one's credibility, dig into one's personal finances, and simply lead to an adverse lifetime memorable experience. After all, your professional opinion has a tremendous impact on people's lives.

Looking at this with a different lens, being an expert can be a very rewarding and fulfilling experience. Yes, it can generate additional revenue, and it can further enhance an individual's credibility. However, to reap more of the benefits of serving as an expert, one must absolutely be prepared to understand the legal system and be ready to perform whatever role they are called upon to serve. While reading this book can assist in such preparation, it is imperative to recognize that one's establishment as an expert is not determined overnight by a single professional accomplishment. In fact, it is based on a career of work, more than likely that of which is built long before one is first asked to be an expert.

In putting together this beginner's guide to being an expert, we have shared some of the basic, yet absolutely essential, components necessary to becoming a credible expert. All experts experience bumps in the road. Those who are least prepared will experience more bumps than others, and they may have been so ill-prepared in their role that they are not asked to serve as an expert ever again. On the contrary, those who take the time to learn, prepare, and treat the role with the importance that it deserves will fare better and earn credibility over time that leads to further expert requests.

Many individuals enjoy "armchair" opinions. At a kitchen table, poolside, or the bar, conversations and debates are found in abundance where people will take one side or another and loudly and proudly state their case. We all enjoy social bantering among friends. In the court of law, it is not a game. Yes, you as an expert must perform, and you must perform well. However, there are much fewer jokes, many more tense moments, and every verbal and/or written word you convey is truly scrutinized from a factual basis. As an expert, your opinions are not based on Google, cable news, or what you overheard at the barbershop or hairdresser. No, your opinions are grounded in evidence, science, standard of care, and expertise. You no longer possess the right to opine on anything you want. Rather, your expertise will be narrowed down for an opinion in a very specialized area. It is no longer about you knowing a little about a lot of things. Instead, you are expected to know a lot about one thing.

In the end, not all experts are truly experts. Yet every lawyer relies on experts for every case to support the facts as they are. So-called bad experts come in all types—inexperienced, egotistical, dull and boring, incompetent, unprofessional, unprepared—and the list goes on. Don't be that person.

It is our sincere hope that this guide serves to help each and every one of you with expert ambitions to hone your skills by taking our advice in learning some of the basic rules of the legal system and the dos and don'ts that we share about the comprehensive process of being an expert witness as a medical and health care provider.

Here's to seeing you in court!

—*Jeff G. Konin, PhD, ATC, PT, FACSM, FNATA*
—*Mark S. Ramey, Esq*

FOREWORD

Over the past 45 years as a trial attorney, I have worked closely with consulting and testifying expert witnesses in federal and state courts around the country. The majority of these cases involved medical and scientific opinions in health care litigation, including medical malpractice, pharmaceutical, and products liability. In their book *Becoming an Expert Witness in Health Care and Litigation: A Beginner's Guide*, Jeff Konin and Mark Ramey provide a comprehensive discussion of important factors for careful consideration by potential expert witnesses and attorneys. Indeed, their subtitle *A Beginner's Guide* is interesting as I believe the overall comprehensive details presented should be well understood by experienced experts and trial counsel. Doing so undoubtedly will assist in achieving successful results.

In their book, the authors pay careful attention to the relevant Federal Rules of Civil Procedure and Federal Rules of Evidence applicable to expert testimony, including medical and scientific evidence. Although variations exist among state court jurisdictions, a thorough understanding of the federal rules and cases is a backbone in health care litigation.

From personal experience, their focus on careful preparation is the sine qua non of successful litigation. As the authors discuss, preparation must start at the very outset and continue throughout all stages of litigation. There is no room for "just winging it" at any stage.

As the authors note, trial judges are the initial "gatekeepers" of individual expert medical and scientific evidence, including expert opinion testimony. Both trial counsel and their retained experts need to fully appreciate the significant role of trial judges in this process and never underestimate the potential ramifications at every stage of litigation. Oftentimes, opposing counsel will test this by way of motions for summary judgment before trial and motions in limine at the start of trial. Again, thorough preparation of the potential expert is crucial.

Most cases that are filed resolve prior to the start of trial. The proper selection of retained experts and careful preparation as discussed by the authors is an important tool in the successful resolution of cases. An important added consideration involves those cases that proceed to trial and jury verdicts. The trial judge will give the jury specific instructions for how they should consider expert testimony. Again, both potential expert witnesses and trial counsel need to appreciate this at the very outset. From personal experience, juries are very adept at weighing the significance of expert testimony presented by both the plaintiff and defendant. The material discussed in the book will be of benefit in achieving successful jury verdicts.

Both authors have considerable hands-on experience in this arena. A thorough appreciation of the materials discussed in their book will be of major assistance to both expert witnesses and trial counsel.

—Eric F. Quandt, JD
Quandt Law
Chicago, Illinois

CHAPTER 1

What Is an Expert?

It is just because civilization is ever evolving, changing, and becoming more complicated that experts find it so difficult to define it in explicit terms.

—Arthur Keith

Chapter Objectives

At the completion of this chapter, you will:
- Understand the distinction between lay and expert testimony
- Identify the prerequisites to qualify as an expert witness
- Recognize the importance of your methodology and reliability of data

Everyone is an expert at something. However, as a medicolegal expert, the issue is whether your opinion will be admissible in a court of law. Your goal is to be known within a professional community as an expert in your chosen field whose opinions are well founded and respected by your peers as well as adversaries, comply with the required foundational elements and rules of procedure, and ultimately are persuasive to a judge or jury.

Konin JG, Ramey MS. *Becoming an Expert Witness in Health Care and Litigation: A Beginner's Guide* (pp 1-4).

You have undergone considerable education, training, and personal experience to gain the expertise within your field and now wish to use that expertise to further your career and increase your income as a retained expert witness for litigation. In order to do so, you must also have an understanding of legal rules and reasoning that ultimately determines the admissibility of your testimony.

Opinions, Inferences, and Expert Testimony

The Federal Rule of Evidence 701 and the Lay Witness

As way of introduction, we begin with the **Federal Rule of Evidence 701**, which provides:

If a witness is not testifying as an expert, the witness's testimony in the form of opinions or inferences is limited to those opinions or inferences that are:

1. rationally based on the perception of the witness,

2. helpful to a clear understanding of the witness's testimony or the determination of a fact in issue, and

3. not based on scientific, technical, or other specialized knowledge within the scope of Rule 702.

Rule 701 was intended to give courts flexibility to allow a lay witness to express themselves through testimony that is arguably opinion by nature but allowed by a lay witness for a more fluid flow of information from the witness to the trier of fact, a judge, or a jury. While this Rule would not be utilized with regard to a professional expert opinion, it helps to understand the underlying thought process of the court and what is intended to be accomplished.

In determining the admissibility of a lay opinion, the courts have formulated a two-prong test that asks the following:

1. Is the opinion rationally based on the perception of the witness?

2. Is the opinion helpful to a clear understanding of the witness's testimony or determination of a fact in issue?

The court commonly interprets this Rule as to permit individuals not qualified as experts but possessing experience or specialized knowledge about particular things to testify about technical matters that might have been thought to lie within the exclusive province of experts. However, when a party proffers a witness expressing an opinion on matters outside of a layperson's perspective or experience, such as the cause of a herniated disc in the lumbar spine or analysis of metal fatigue contributing to the collapse of a building, the admissibility of the opinion will likely shift in scope to Federal Rule of Evidence 702.

The Federal Rule of Evidence 702 and the Expert Witness

The **Federal Rule of Evidence 702** requires the proponent of expert testimony to:

1. produce a witness who is "qualified" to offer opinions in the subject matter of his or her proffered testimony and
2. the proffered testimony must help the jury to understand the evidence or to decide a fact at issue in the case.

If scientific, technical, or other specialized knowledge will assist the trier of fact to understand the evidence or to determine a fact in issue, a witness qualified as an expert by knowledge, skill, experience, training, or education may testify thereto in the form of an opinion or otherwise if:

1. the testimony is based on sufficient facts or data,
2. the testimony is the product of reliable principles and methods, and
3. the witness has applied the principles and methods reliably to the facts of the case.

Rule 702 is one of four Rules of Evidence directly applicable to an evaluation of the admissibility of your expert testimony.

The Federal Rule of Evidence 703 and Reliability of Data

The **Federal Rule of Evidence 703** requires that experts base their testimony on reliable facts and data, which requires the court to make "an independent evaluation of the reliability of the data" underlying the expert opinion.

The facts or data in the particular case upon which an expert bases an opinion or inference may be those perceived by or made known to the expert at or before the hearing. If of a type reasonably relied upon by experts in the particular field informing opinions or inferences upon the subject, the facts or data need not be admissible in evidence in order for the opinion or inference to be admitted. Facts or data that are otherwise inadmissible shall not be disclosed to the jury by the proponent of the opinion or inference unless the Court determines that their probative value in assisting the jury to evaluate the expert's opinion substantially outweighs their prejudicial affect.

The Rule expressly permits an expert witness to base their opinion on inadmissible evidence as long as these facts or data are of a type reasonably relied upon by experts in the particular field informing opinions or inferences upon the subject.

While Rule 702 focuses on the expert's methodology, Rule 703 focuses on the data underlying the expert's opinion.

The Federal Rule of Evidence 403 and Exclusion

The **Federal Rule of Evidence 403** authorizes the exclusion of any relevant testimony "if its probative value is substantially outweighed by the danger of unfair prejudice, confusion of the issues, or misleading the jury."

The assessment of whether proffered expert testimony is admissible is a preliminary question for the court under **Federal Rule of Evidence 104(a)**, which provides that "preliminary questions concerning the qualification of a person to be a witness, . . . or the admissibility of evidence shall be determined by the Court."

While a license or formal education may be helpful in qualifying as an expert in your field, neither is strictly necessary pursuant to the rules. However, while enhancing your credibility, it is most often a prerequisite of the client seeking your expert opinion.

Expert testimony itself is generally required by the court when the subject matter to be resolved by the jury is so particularly related to science, technology, or a profession that it is beyond the understanding of the average layperson. Thus, tort and contract cases involving complex scientific or technical principles will usually require expert testimony.

A court's decision to admit expert testimony is governed by an abuse of discretion standard. The issue as to whether expert testimony is required to prosecute a certain claim is governed by state law.

While courts have declined to issue broad proclamations as to what cases or situations require expert testimony, the number of cases finding such testimony unnecessary is fewer than those requiring it, and the practicing attorney would be wise to resolve any doubts in favor of retaining an expert and introducing their testimony.

CHAPTER 2

Qualifications of an Expert

Now I'm a scientific expert; that means I know nothing about absolutely everything.

—Arthur C. Clarke

Chapter Objectives

At the completion of this chapter, you will:

- Become familiar with the two-prong test for admissibility of your opinions
- Recognize the key factors that challenge expert testimony

While the Federal Rules of Evidence provide for the elements or "hurdles" necessary for qualification as an expert witness and admissibility of your opinions, as an expert witness, you must be familiar with case law relied upon by the courts, which further interpret the Rules of Evidence and their application.

Every matter in which you may be called upon to provide opinion will likely differ factually and opinions legally challenged as not meeting one or more of the required elements. While the party retaining your services seeks to ensure compliance with the Rules, the opposing party will likely argue the expert does not possess the necessary qualifications for providing an opinion within the field of inquiry or the opinion is not based upon the appropriate standard of evidentiary reliability or trustworthiness.

Konin JG, Ramey MS. *Becoming an Expert Witness in Health Care and Litigation: A Beginner's Guide* (pp 5-8).

DAUBERT

Without doubt, and given time, your opinions will be subject to a *Daubert* motion. The seminal case relied upon to challenge expert opinion arises from *Daubert v. Merrell Dow Pharmaceuticals*. In this matter, the Supreme Court and Ninth Circuit interpreted the Federal Rules of Evidence and outlined the criteria the federal courts must use in assessing the admissibility of challenged expert testimony under Rule 702.

UNDERSTANDING OF *DAUBERT* AND ITS KEY FACTORS, ADMISSIBILITY OF YOUR OPINIONS

Prior to the enactment of Rule 702 in 1975, the admissibility of expert testimony was governed by the "general acceptance" standard. In the matter of *Frye v. United States*, a convicted murderer appealed his conviction on the grounds that he should have been allowed to introduce evidence of a primitive form of a lie detector test (ie, systolic blood pressure deception test). The court concluded that the test had not yet gained such general scientific acceptance and affirmed the conviction.

After the enactment of the Federal Rules of Evidence in 1975, the courts struggled with the apparent conflict between the *Frye* "general acceptance" standard and the language provided by the rules. In 1993, the Supreme Court addressed these issues in **Daubert**, concluding that the court, or judge, will serve as a "gatekeeper" to ensure consistency and that "any and all scientific testimony or evidence admitted is not only relevant, but reliable."

The matter of *Daubert* involved a claim that the antinausea drug Bendectin had caused reduced-limb birth defects in infants whose mothers had taken the drug to combat morning sickness during pregnancy.

TWO-PRONG TEST

In its analysis of Rule 702, the Supreme Court established a **two-prong test** to assist trial judges in assessing a proffer of your expert scientific testimony:

1. "The subject of an expert's testimony must be scientific knowledge."

The court further explained:

The adjective "scientific" implies a grounding in the methods and procedures of science. Similarly, the word "knowledge" connotes more than subjective belief or unsupported speculation. The term "applies to any body of known facts or to any body of ideas inferred from such facts or accepted as truths on good grounds" . . . proposed testimony must be supported by appropriate validation ie, "good grounds," based on what is known.

2. The expert testimony must "assist" the trier of fact further characterized as "relevant to the task at hand" in that it "logically advances a material aspect of the proposing party's case."

Key Factors

Both the Supreme Court and various circuits have identified factors to be considered when ruling on a challenge to proffered expert testimony. The following, while not exhaustive, provides insight as to the court's inquiry or thought process when determining the admissibility of your opinions.

- Did the expert base their opinions on prior, independent research, or were the opinions generally solely for use in litigation?
- If the testimony arose from litigation work, are the theories underlying the opinions generally accepted within the relevant scientific community?
- If the theories are not "generally accepted," did the expert at least subject the theories to peer review and publication?
- If the expert did not subject their work to peer review and publication, was the expert employing a "standard" scientific methodology in arriving at their conclusions?
- If the expert did not use an accepted methodology, was the theory tested and/or was it susceptible to testing by others?
- If the theory was, or could be, tested, what was the known or potential rate of error in the expert's analysis?

More likely than not, you will be retained as an expert witness by legal counsel representing either the plaintiff or the defendant involved in civil litigation seeking monetary damages. While expert testimony is sought to provide opinions in support of the party that has retained you, with the goal of persuading a jury of laypersons at trial, the basis of your opinions will be considered by the court to determine their admissibility based upon compliance with the Rules of Evidence and their interpretation by the court. A basic understanding of the legal inquiry will be essential in furthering your opinions and continued retention as an expert.

In summation, anticipate the court to make a preliminary assessment of whether the reasoning or methodology underlying the testimony is scientifically valid and whether that reasoning or methodology properly can be applied to the facts at issue. It is important to understand that the courts will analyze not what you the expert says but what basis you have for saying it.

The burden of proving the admissibility of your opinion will fall squarely on the party that retained you as a proponent of the scientific evidence. As found in *Daubert*, the court determined that the plaintiff failed to meet the second prong of Rule 702 in that their expert could not establish at least a doubling of risk from Bendectin ingestion, and therefore, their opinions would not actually assist the jury in determining a fact at issue and in fact would tend to disprove legal causation, under a more probable than not standard.

The courts continue to apply the reasoning of *Daubert* and its subsequent interpretations to expert opinions throughout the various courts in the United States. While the factors listed in *Daubert* are helpful, the Court has gone to great lengths to emphasize that the Rule 702 inquiry is a flexible one. The applicability of the factors listed in *Daubert* can neither be ruled in nor ruled out for any particular case. The trial court maintains latitude in determining whether your expert testimony is sufficiently relevant and reliable for admission into evidence.

Chapter 3

The Role of an Expert

An expert knows all the answers, if you ask the right questions.
—Levi Strauss

Chapter Objectives

At the completion of this chapter, you will:

- Appreciate the pros and cons of retention by the plaintiff vs defendant
- Differentiate between your objective opinions vs "what you think they want"
- Understand considerations of anticipated discovery

CONSIDERATIONS AS TO WHICH "SIDE" OR PARTY YOU WANT TO "PLAY" FOR

Regardless of whether you have been **retained** as a consulting or testifying expert, you should be knowledgeable and consider the distinctions between retention by the party bringing the claim, in civil matters known as the **plaintiff**, and the party that denies or defends the claim (ie, the **defendant**). In criminal matters, the government (ie, federal or state) will be prosecuting criminal charges against a criminal defendant.

Konin JG, Ramey MS. *Becoming an Expert Witness in Health Care and Litigation: A Beginner's Guide* (pp 9-14).

Typically, over time, an expert will become known within the legal community as favoring one side over the other, largely dependent upon the nature of the expert's practice or track record evidencing the number of times retained by either side.

An expert may be an interested party when providing services to a plaintiff typically as a treating physician for injuries sustained in a negligence action. Otherwise, the expert witness would be directly retained by either party to provide opinions.

Pros and Cons of Retention by Plaintiff Versus Defendant

As a treating physician, the medical expert has already entered into an agreement with the patient and/or their legal counsel, for payment or compensation for their services. The majority of medical professionals accept various insurance coverages and receive payment for services pursuant to varied fee schedules established by a health insurance carrier or federal program such as Medicare. These fee schedules typically provide compensation for each itemized procedure or service provided but at a reduced or fraction of the original charge (Figure 3-1).

Direct Retention by the Parties

Most often an expert will be approached by a litigant to assist with evaluation of their respective position and retain you for consulting services and/or expert testimony. In these matters, the expert is retained directly by legal counsel on behalf of the party represented. A contract is utilized in this scenario, prepared, and used uniformly by the expert, which sets forth the parameters of retention and various fee schedules for services anticipated to be provided.

In civil litigation, many medical providers choose to enter into contractual agreements with a patient's legal counsel, often referred to as **letter of protection**, on behalf of the plaintiff. Typically, this is a simple one- or two-page form signed by the medical professional, patient, and legal counsel that promises to pay for medical care through proceeds of the litigation. The advantage is the potential to receive 100% payment of the provider's bill upon the conclusion of litigation. The disadvantage often concerns a less-than-favorable legal verdict or result requiring apportionment of the award among multiple providers. Many consider the potential reward to outweigh the risk and/or provide in their letter of protection that regardless of the outcome, the patient remains responsible for the total amount of bill.

In the alternative, your expert opinion may be sought on behalf of the defendant. Payment for your services will likely be based upon an hourly rate for specific services.

JOHN SMITH, MD *Board Certifications*	Address City, State, Zip Telephone Number	
Legal Fee Schedule		
Attorney Consultation	30 minutes	$500.00
Deposition—nonwork comp (prepaid)	1 hour	$1,500.00
	For every additional 30 minutes	$600.00
Deposition—work comp (prepaid)	1 hour	$1,000.00
	For every additional hour	$450.00
Deposition—video recorded (prepaid)	1 hour	$2,000.00
IME—nonwork comp (prepaid)		$1,500.00
X-rays will be an additional charge		
Record review will be an additional charge		
IME—work comp (prepaid)		$1,200.00
X-rays will be an additional charge		
Record review will be an additional charge		
Trial Appearance	Half day	$4,500.00
	Full day	$9,000.00
Medical Record Review (billed based on time; records must be emailed or delivered in CD or flash drive)		TBD
Additional charge per hour	1 hour	$400.00
Record Review—nonwork comp and work comp	1 hour	$1,000.00
Additional charge per hour	1 hour	$400.00
C30A form		$250.00
Questionnaire		$250.00
Deposition/trial fees are nonrefundable as our physicians have set aside time out of their schedule to accommodate these requests. Any other services listed above are nonrefundable if cancelled or not rescheduled within 7 business days of original appointment.		
All prepaid services must be paid 5 business days prior to scheduled appointment. No electronic payments will be accepted. Live checks must be mailed to the address above.		

Figure 3-1. Example fee schedule.

Typically, the retained expert establishes a **fee schedule** including but not limited to the following:

- Conferences
- Nonvideo depositions, 2-hour minimum
- Video depositions, with 2-hour minimum
- Records review, cost based on "thickness of records"
- Supplemental/excess record review
- Diagnostic test/film review
- Deposition transcript review
- Review of surgical video
- Rehabilitation notes
- Trial attendance, 4- or 8-hour block
- Independent medical exam/compulsory medical exam or second opinion
- Expedite fee

The charges for these various services are established by you the expert and often based upon comparison with your competition. As an expert, your retainer agreement and fee schedule will also likely contain specific procedures for submission of information and/or scheduling to be complied with by the counsel that has retained you. Much of this will be discussed in greater detail in Chapter 8 of this book.

Significantly, defense counsel has usually been retained by an institutional client, such as an insurance company, which may ultimately be responsible for the payment of damages awarded through litigation.

As such, prepayment for your services is standard and the risk of nonpayment minimal.

YOUR ROLE

The role of an expert is to provide advice or opinions on matters within your field of expertise. The expert must realize that their opinions will be challenged by opposing experts in your field, as well as legally through opposing counsel, who possess greater knowledge of the Rules of Evidence and legal opinions, which ultimately affect admissibility of your opinions and reputation.

Often, a retained expert will attempt to slant their opinion in favor of the party who has retained their services. This is typically done by omitting facts or complete analysis.

Your role as an expert will be simplified by focusing solely on your field of expertise and allowing the attorney to be the lawyer. The best advice is "you be the doctor, let the lawyer be the lawyer."

YOUR REPUTATION

While your role as a retained expert will likely be profitable, you should consider the several frustrating and often stressful realities that you will be subject to.

Your opinions will be challenged and often involve a lengthy deposition or cross-examination in preparation for the hearing or trial. The competency of the legal counsel involved will vary depending upon the years of experience. The line of questioning will range from simple inquiries as to your ultimate conclusions to complex, frustrating, and stressful lines of in-depth questions.

Quite often, the attorney will begin the inquiry with questions concerning your underlying and continuing education and/or accomplishments vs your published curriculum vitae in an attempt to discredit you. Transcripts of previous testimony will also be used to determine consistency of your opinions vs impeachment of them when in conflict. You will be challenged on your knowledge of the specific facts and their application to the basis of your opinions.

A WORD OF ADVICE

In lieu of "playing" for one side or the other, the most successful experts can provide opinions for both.

In the beginning of your career as a retained expert, you must start somewhere. Through your marketing efforts, or simply word of mouth, an interested party has approached you for advice or opinion. You will likely be tempted to provide them with an opinion consistent with their stated goal of prosecuting or defending against monetary damages. In so doing, you seek to assist them in maximizing their case as well as your potential for repeat business and/or referrals to others.

A common mistake for new consulting or testifying experts is making assumptions about unknown facts and/or providing ultimate opinions without consideration as to evidence or facts that undermine that opinion. If retained as a testifying expert, your opinions will necessarily be reduced to writing in a report required to be produced to the opposing counsel. An experienced trial counsel will likely cross-examine you through deposition and more likely than not have educated themselves on the subject matter, consulted their own experts, and identified the missing facts and/or weakness in the basis of your opinions.

Sound advice is to provide the most thorough and objective analysis and reasoning in support of your opinion. Upon questioning during cross-examination, maintain objectivity in light of the facts presented and respond as appropriate within your field of expertise as opposed to what the lawyer would necessarily like to hear.

A well-reasoned, factual, and analytical basis for your position will continue to enhance your credibility and reputation throughout your career.

YOUR FINANCES

Last but not least, you should be aware and take into consideration that your business and/or personal finances may also be subject to inquiry and disseminated to third parties or the public at trial.

Dependent upon whether you have been qualified as an expert due to your status as a treating physician or directly retained by an interested party, litigation will often involve written requests for documentation concerning the financial arrangement you have entered into with the retaining party. This information is often determined to be relevant in legal proceedings as to the issue of bias. The inquiry typically requests information concerning not only the current litigation but your involvement in litigation for a period of years. The inquiry will concern not only the amount of money received from the party that has retained you but also the amount of money earned from all sources in your capacity as an expert witness. The courts often require the expert witness to maintain ongoing records in anticipation of this discovery request.

CHAPTER 4

Preparation for Expert Opinions

There are as many opinions as there are experts.
—Franklin D. Roosevelt

Chapter Objectives

At the completion of this chapter, you will:
- Distinguish privileges that apply to consulting vs testifying experts
- Identify documents and issues necessary for evaluation of injury
- Become familiar with the issue of spoliation of evidence

BEFORE LITIGATION, CONSULTANT VERSUS TESTIFYING EXPERT

Within the medicolegal community of experts, there is typically an initiating traumatic event, or **date of loss**, which is alleged to have legally caused the injury and resulting damages sought. The interested parties, commonly the plaintiff or injured party, the defendant or allegedly negligent party, and/or insurance carrier, have been placed on notice shortly after the occurrence of the event.

The injured party will quite often be represented by counsel who presents a demand to an insurance carrier for damages with supporting documentation in support of the same. In complex matters, the insurance carrier often retains defense counsel to

Konin JG, Ramey MS. *Becoming an Expert Witness in Health Care and Litigation: A Beginner's Guide* (pp 15-23).
© 2023 SLACK Incorporated.

EXPERT REQUEST TO PRODUCE

1. Any documents, papers, tapes, photographs, statements, or anything received or reviewed by the expert from any source in connection with their expert testimony in this case.

2. A copy of the expert's résumé, CV, or any other document or thing indicating their background, education, or experience.

3. Any document, retainer, agreement, contract, letter, or any other paper indicating the basis of their retention as an expert in this case.

4. Any handwritten note, photographs, tapes, videotapes, graphs, charts, diagrams, or any other paper, document, or anything generated by the expert in connection with this case.

5. All reports, papers, documents, memos, or any other paper or anything indicating all opinions, proposed opinion, "rough opinion," or any other opinions you have, have had, or may have in this case.

6. Any papers, memos, notes, diagrams, photographs, tapes, videotapes, or other papers, documents, or things indicating or evidencing the examination, inspection, testing, or review of the [subject matter], product, or scene of the [type of incident] involved in this case.

7. Any papers, memos, diagrams, reports, or any other paper or thing indicating their findings with regard to any inspection, testing, examination, or other review of the [subject matter], if applicable, or scene of the [type of incident] involved in this case.

8. All documents, papers, or things indicating facts the expert received about the [subject matter], product, or scene of the [type of incident] involved in this case from any source or entity.

9. All statements, interrogatories, depositions, or other court discovery reviewed by the expert in connection with their testimony in this case.

Figure 4-1. Expert request to produce. (*continued*)

evaluate the claim and request additional documentation and/or employ the appropriate experts to assist in the evaluation (Figure 4-1).

The attorney representing the injured party may actually refer the client to you as a patient, and therefore, you may become an expert treating physician and/or health care provider. Or in the alternative, either party may seek to retain your services as a **consulting or testifying expert.**

Your initial conference with the retaining party will identify your role as a consultant who will never be asked to testify, a consultant who may be asked to testify at a later date, or a designated expert with the anticipation that you will provide sworn testimony via deposition or trial. It is not always immediately obvious at the outset of retention but certainly a topic of discussion due to the different rules of privilege that may apply.

10. Any books, pamphlets, circulars, treatises, or any other book or periodical relied upon or reviewed by the expert in preparing to testify or utilize in any manner in connection with their expert testimony in this case.

11. Any advertisements, circulars, or any other documents, papers, or things utilized by the expert in advertising or presenting their services to the public for hire.

12. All bills, papers, memos, or documents that indicate when the expert was first retained in this case.

13. All bills, papers, memos, or documents that indicate the total amount of time the expert has spent and what has been done for each increment of time charges from the time they were first retained to the present.

14. Any models, charts, tapes, video, or any other paper or thing that will be utilized by the expert to explain or otherwise illustrate to the jury any of their opinions or testimony in this case.

15. All telephone memos, documents, papers, correspondence, or any other thing indicating communication with any other person other than plaintiff's attorney or entity regarding this case.

16. Any documents, papers, or things indicating any other investigation, research, or work that the expert intends to do, or has been instructed to do, or desired to be done subsequent to their deposition in this case.

17. All cards, papers, or things indicating the number of cases the expert currently has open on behalf of the law firm that retained them in this case.

18. The expert's entire file regarding this case excluding correspondence with retaining attorneys and including a copy of any and all documents and bills reflecting services rendered, the amount charged for the services, and payments made for the services.

19. All catalogues, memos, or any other paper or things indicating the expert's comparison of the product in this case with those of other manufacturers.

Figure 4-1 (continued). Expert request to produce.

As a consulting expert, your opinion may be useful in determining legal issues that often involve whether injuries were caused or aggravated by the traumatic event at issue or some other cause such as medical malpractice. Biomechanical experts may render opinions concerning whether the necessary resulting force of impact or mechanism of injury is present and consistent with the injury. A biomechanist may be employed to provide opinions concerning the timing and sequence of events, which may assist in determination of negligence. Experts in sports medicine may determine if preexisting conditions or circumstances may have led to a more serious (including catastrophic) injury.

Figure 4-2. Example of a faulty raised sprinkler system that may have led to a knee injury on a field.

DIFFERENT PRIVILEGE RULES APPLY

If retained as a testifying expert, all information that you have considered in forming your opinions must potentially be disclosed pursuant to **Federal Rule of Civil Procedure 26(a)(2)(B).**

As a consulting expert, your involvement may never be disclosed to a third party. For a consulting/nontestifying expert, disclosure of information relied upon would require "exceptional circumstances" that make it "impractical" to obtain information from any other way, per the **Federal Rule of Civil Procedure 26(b)(4)(B).**

When a consultant becomes a testifying expert, disclosure usually requires anything considered after the initial retention.

PRESUIT ANALYSIS AND RECORDS REVIEW

Following retention, you may expect to receive documentation or a package of background materials to facilitate a substantive discussion and/or upon which you have been directed to review and provide opinions, referred to as **presuit analysis**. The materials will vary from case to case but typically include items similar to the following:

- Photographs depicting the scene of incident and/or injuries (Figure 4-2)
- Medical records from treating physicians/providers
- Employment records

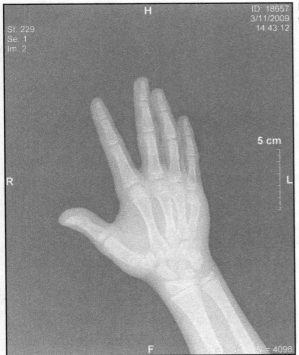

Figure 4-3. Diagnostic images of a wrist and hand injury.

- Diagnostic studies (Figure 4-3)
- Deposition transcripts and/or statements of parties or witnesses
- Reports of other experts of various specialties

INTERVIEW AND CONSULTATION

Following receipt of your initial materials, you should anticipate a conference with the retaining counsel to discuss the following:

- If not already known, you should have provided a curriculum vitae to the retaining counsel and be prepared to discuss your education, training, and experience in both your field of expertise and litigation
- General as well as specific facts giving rise to the alleged injury
- Subjective complaints
- Documented objective findings on examination throughout the course of care and treatment
- Findings on diagnostic studies
- Correlation of subjective complaints with objective findings and diagnostic studies

- Diagnosis related to symptomology
- Relationship of diagnosis to the traumatic incident at issue
- Any/all peer-reviewed or accepted treatises or professional studies done or in support of your opinion

PRELIMINARY OPINIONS

When retained as a consulting expert, you should inquire as to whether the client is seeking a verbal or written opinion, known as a **preliminary opinion**. This is determined on a case-by-case basis and may also involve consideration as to cost or expense involved in drafting a formal report.

However, more importantly, the party requesting your opinion would likely appreciate a verbal opinion or heads-up if the preliminary opinion is adverse to their position. Remember, dependent upon the nature of your retention and possible other factors, an adverse opinion that has been reduced to writing may be discoverable.

IN LITIGATION, THE DISCOVERY PROCESS

In many instances, you will be retained during the legal proceedings. When retained as a testifying expert, you will be subject to the legal **discovery** process.

Discovery directed to experts may involve one or more of the following:

- Interrogatories
- Request for production
- Deposition

Following your disclosure as an expert in the matter, you can anticipate the opposing counsel will propound written discovery in the form of interrogatories and a request for production (Figure 4-4).

The inquiry will concern your background, education, training, and experience, as well as opinions and basis for your opinions. Information will also be sought to consider any bias of your opinion to include your retention agreement, fee agreement/schedule, and income received on the subject matter. Unfortunately, the inquiry will go further in seeking information concerning other matters in which the retaining counsel has employed you previously, as well as your retention and income related to your expert retention overall. The courts usually allow inquiry of you and/or your business's received income over the previous 4 to 5 years. This usually includes an ongoing list of clients and/or cases in which you have been retained, the style of the case in litigation, the attorney involved, whether retained by the plaintiff or defendant, and amounts of payments received in connection with the same.

EXPERT INTERROGATORIES

1. Identify by name, business address, profession, and specialty each expert witness you intend to call at trial.

2. State the scope of employment of each expert witness in the pending case. Please identify each instance in which the plaintiff or plaintiff's counsel has hired, retained, or paid money to each expert witness disclosed above to provide expert opinions, examinations, or testimony within the last three (3) years.

3. For each expert witness disclosed above, please state the standard rate of compensation sought by the expert in this case, as well as the amount sought for the following duties:

   a. Records review.

   b. Medical or property examination.

   c. Deposition testimony.

   d. Trial testimony.

4. For each expert witness disclosed above, state whether the expert generally performs work on behalf of the plaintiff or the defendant. Please also state the percentage of expert work each performs on behalf of the plaintiff and the defendant.

5. For each expert witness disclosed above, state what percentage of professional time is devoted to service as an expert.

6. Please identify every case, by style, case number, and court, in which each expert disclosed above has testified as an expert, either by deposition or at trial, for the past three (3) years. As to each identified case, please also state whether the testimony was by deposition or at trial, or both, and whether the testimony was on behalf of the plaintiff or the defendant.

7. Please state the total amount of money received by the expert in the last three (3) years for expert services, including but not limited to opinions, depositions, and testimony, for services provided in the capacity as a medical examiner or expert witness.

8. For each expert witness identified above, please list all documents, materials, letters, or opinions, as to any matters referenced in their opinions regarding digital motion X-rays, including AMA publications, Current Procedural Terminology assistance opinions and publications, CPT Advisory Panel findings, CPT Information Services findings, and copies of communications between patient care technicians and private providers/insurers or any documents pertaining to the private communications.

9. For each expert witness identified above, please list all documents, materials, letters, or opinions, as to any matters referenced in their opinions.

Figure 4-4. Example expert interrogatories.

The courts have entered rulings related to your role as an expert treating physician or health care provider as well, when providing services pursuant to a letter of protection or dependent upon the outcome of the litigation. Following receipt of this paper discovery, if the matter is proceeding to hearing or trial, the opposing counsel will schedule your deposition in preparation. The length of the deposition will vary, but you could be safe in assuming a 2-hour minimum. During cross-examination, questioning by the opposing counsel will rely heavily upon the documents you have produced and provide the foundation for much of the questioning as to your qualifications and for your opinions.

EXAMINATIONS

Dependent upon your field of expertise, reason for retention, and whether retained on behalf of the plaintiff as the injured party or the defendant, in defense of the claim, you may be required to examine the injured party, site of event, or object/subject of the litigation. The injured party or plaintiff may retain you for a second opinion to a treating physician concerning diagnosis or necessitation for future medical care/ life care plan. If retained on behalf of the defendant, you may be asked to perform an independent or compulsory medical exam.

In both circumstances, you will likely be required to write a written report that details your findings, opinions, and recommendations. With regard to the examination on behalf of the defense, you will be governed by federal, state, and/or local rules of court as to how the examination is to be conducted to include parties that can be present, documents or records to be produced, and the timing of disclosure of your opinions.

Regardless as to the requesting party, you must be aware of and compliant with the Rules of Procedure. The counsel retaining you for your services will be responsible for advising you as to the requirements and adherence to the same.

By the time of drafting your report, you should have a common understanding with retaining counsel of what the pertinent issues are and analysis of those issues.

Be cognizant of court opinions that cite expert overreliance on attorney information as a reason for finding discoverable, otherwise privileged attorney/work product contained within your files. If an adverse party is able to determine the extent to which your opinion has been shaped or influenced by the version of facts selected and presented by the retaining counsel, the court may determine that the attorney must have access to the documents and materials that you have considered. Without such access, the opposing party will be unable to conduct a full and fair cross-examination.

SPOLIATION

It is well settled that a party that reasonably anticipates litigation has an affirmative duty to preserve relevant evidence. Experts, as agents, likewise have a duty to preserve evidence and to exercise reasonable care in the handling of evidence. Sanctions for **spoliation of evidence** include a negative inference instruction to the jury, preclusion of the issue, and outright dismissal of the case.

The expert should be aware of, and avoid, the possibility of destructive testing (ie, where the very test may result in destroying a critical item or in rendering further inspection or testing of it useless for purposes of the litigation). Such testing should be avoided whenever possible if the opposing party has not been given an opportunity to participate.

Even the fact that you may have preserved portions of the relevant items may not be sufficient to avoid sanctions if the court finds that the portions preserved are insufficient for the opposing party to utilize to rebut your opinion or if destructive testing was in fact not necessary.

Numerous courts have ordered the exclusion of expert testimony concerning a relevant item of evidence due to the destruction, loss, or alteration of the item, or they have ordered the total exclusion of any evidence concerning the condition of the item. If the plaintiff is the party precluded, such a ruling will often have the effect of preventing them from making a prima facie case, or if the defendant is precluded, they may be unable to offer any evidence to rebut the plaintiff's case.

CHAPTER 5

Disclosure of Opinions, Basis, and Bias

Without the opinion of an expert, there's no such thing as certainty.

—Joanna Ruocco

Chapter Objectives

At the completion of this chapter, you will:

- Understand the distinction and privileges provided to consulting vs testifying experts
- Identify practical discovery concerns as an expert witness
- Comprehend the governing rules and requirements of your expert report

Dependent upon the nature of your retention, either as a consulting expert or as a testifying expert, the disclosure of your opinions and/or file contents will differ.

The underlying concept concerns the fact that as a consulting expert, the original intent was to provide advice or opinions to a retained party not intended to be disseminated to others vs a testifying expert where the intent is ultimately to provide persuasive testimony/opinions to the fact finder.

Konin JG, Ramey MS. *Becoming an Expert Witness in
Health Care and Litigation: A Beginner's Guide* (pp 25-36).
© 2023 SLACK Incorporated.

CONSULTING EXPERTS

When retained as an expert, Federal Rule of Civil Procedure 26(b)(4)(B) provides: A party may discover facts known or opinions held by an expert who has been retained or specifically employed by another party in anticipation of litigation or preparation for trial and who is not expected to be called as a witness at trial, only . . . upon showing of exceptional circumstances under which it is impracticable for the party seeking discovery to obtain facts or opinions on the same subject by any other means.

In addition to this Rule, the cases interpreting the same have generally held that the identity and location of a consultant who is not expected to testify at trial are not subject to discovery except upon a showing of exceptional circumstances.

What is determined to be "an exceptional circumstance" again is determined on a case-by-case and factual basis. As an example, the following two illustrations provide insight:

- The object or condition at issue was destroyed or unavailable after the consulting expert sought and before the movant's expert had an opportunity to examine.
- No other experts were available in the particular field.

TESTIFYING EXPERTS

Once an expert is disclosed as an expert witness, the general rule is that anything contained in their files is fair game for discovery. A number of jurisdictions subscribe to the Rule that privileged materials, especially those that contain the opinion work product of counsel, are protected from discovery. Because the law in this area is often unsettled, one should presume that anything contained in the expert's file may some-day be produced and discovered.

EXPERTS RELYING UPON THE WORK OF OTHER EXPERTS

In some matters, multiple experts are retained, and it is necessary for one or more to rely upon the work of another. If retained as a testifying expert and relying upon the work of a consulting expert, the consulting expert file may be subject to discovery. In such cases, it is recommended that the testifying expert conduct an independent analysis or review of the consulting expert's work. It is critical that the testifying expert apply their knowledge to the facts and create their own opinion, as the testifying expert may not simply be a conduit for another expert in the matter.

EXPERTS RELYING ONLY UPON INFORMATION PROVIDED BY AN ATTORNEY

As a testifying expert, you should avoid basing opinions on information obtained from the retained attorney only. Due to the associated time and expense, legal counsel may determine it to be cheaper and easier to screen information that you receive. Experienced opposing counsel will ultimately inquire as to the basis and source of information relied upon and, if solely on legal counsel, will proceed with a fertile and effective cross-examination.

Documents and information disclosed to a testifying expert in connection with their testimony are discoverable by the opposing party, whether or not the expert relies on the documents and information in preparing their report. The courts generally find that disclosure of attorney/client communications or work product to an expert results in a waiver of this privilege.

EXPERT WITNESS REPORT

In a federal proceeding, **Federal Rule of Civil Procedure 26(a)(2)(A)** requires a party to disclose the identity of any potential trial witness who will give expert testimony, and a report is only required with respect to "a witness who is retained or specially employed to provide expert testimony in the case or whose duties as an employee of the party regularly involved giving expert testimony."

Federal Rule of Civil Procedure 26(a)(2)(C) specifies that such reports are due no later than 90 days prior to trial, except for rebuttal evidence, which is due 30 days after the opponent's disclosures have been made.

Federal Rule of Civil Procedure 26(a)(2)(B) provides for the information that must be included in your report, which you should be familiar with as follows (Figure 5-1):

1. a complete statement of all opinions to be expressed and the reasons and basis underlying the opinions,

2. the data or other information considered by the witness in forming the opinions,

3. any exhibits to be used as a summary of or support for the opinions,

4. the qualifications of the witness, including a list of all publications authored by the witness within the past 10 years,

5. the compensation to be paid for the study and testimony, and

6. a list of any other cases in which the witness has testified as an expert at trial or by deposition within the preceding 4 years.

JOHN SMITH, MD
Board Certifications
Address, City, State, Zip
Phone

COMPULSORY MEDICAL EXAMINATION
(Neurology)

DATE:

COMPLETE HISTORY AND PHYSICAL

RE: Examinee Name:

    Examinee DOB:

This examination was performed with a videographer as well as claimant's attorney present. The patient was notified that this is a compulsory medical examination, that I am not a treating physician, and that if examinee had any symptoms or issues during the exam, the examinee should notify me immediately.

Chief Complaint:

History of Chief Complaint:

Past Medical History:

Social History:

Occupation:

Current Medications:

Allergies:

Family History:

Review of Symptoms:

Constitution Symptoms:
Eyes:
Ear, Nose, Mouth, and Throat:
Cardiovascular:
Respiratory:
Gastrointestinal:
Genitourinary:
Musculoskeletal:
Integumentary (Skin and/or Breast):
Neurological:
Psychiatric:
Endocrine:

Figure 5-1. Examples of an expert report. (*continued*)

Hematologic/Lymphatic:

Allergic/Immunologic:

Physical Examination:

Height:

Weight:

Blood Pressure:

Pulse:

Cervical Spine:

Thoracic Spine:

Lumbar Spine:

Upper Extremities:

Lower Extremities:

Neurological Examination:

Mental Status:

Gait:

Pupils:

Cranial Nerves:

Cerebellar:

Cortical:

Motor Examination:

Sensory Examination:

Reflexes:

Medical Records/Imaging Review:

Impression:

Opinions:

Maximum Medical and Surgical Improvement:

Further Diagnostic Testing:

Further Treatment:

Regular Work Activities, Restrictions, or Limitations:

Permanent Injury:

Imaging Shows:

I declare that the information contained within this report was prepared and is the work and product of the undersigned, John Smith, MD, and is true to the best of my knowledge and information.

[Signature Block]

Figure 5-1 (continued). Examples of an expert report. (*continued*)

JOHN SMITH, MD
Board Certifications
Address, City, State, Zip
Phone

COMPULSORY MEDICAL EVALUATION

Date of CME Examination:

Referring Attorney, Name and Address:

Name of Examinee: Doe, Jane.

Date of Loss:

Dear (Referring Attorney):

As discussed with the examinee, today's visit is for a Compulsory Medical Evaluation.

A medical history, physical examination, review of available records, and review of submitted diagnostic studies will result in this report. All of the opinions are based on the information that is provided to the date of this report.

All of the opinions are based on a reasonable degree of medical probability.

There is no establishment of a patient–physician relationship. While a history is obtained, and a physical exam is performed, no counseling about treatment options or diagnosis will be offered to the examinee.

Medical complaints not related to [specialty] may be acknowledged but no expert opinions will be offered on these complaints.

The examinee was accompanied by a videographer, who filmed the encounter. Examinee was informed that videography was arranged by their own legal representative.

By records or questioning, the examinee was being represented by [attorney] at the time of the evaluation. Examination was also conducted in the presence of the examinee's legal counsel at the time of the evaluation.

Face-to-Face Time:

Records Submitted for Review:

HISTORY

Chief Complaint:

Current VAS Pain Scale:

Figure 5-1 (continued). Examples of an expert report. (*continued*)

HISTORY OF CHIEF COMPLAINTS

Current Pain Medication:

Current Physical Limitations:

Past Musculoskeletal/Neurological Conditions:

Past Medical History:

Past Surgical History:

Social History:

Occupational History:

PHYSICAL EXAMINATION

HT: **WT:**

Gait: **Sitting Posture:**

Cervical Spine

Palpation:

Range of Motion:

Thoracic Spine

Palpation:

Range of Motion:

Lumbar Spine

Palpation:

Range of Motion:

Motor Exam:

Sensory Exam:

LE Reflexes:

SLR:

FABER: **Clonus:**

Hip Exam:

Knee and LE Exam:

Figure 5-1 (continued). Examples of an expert report. (*continued*)

Neurological Examination

Motor Exam:

Sensory Exam:

Deep Tendon Reflexes:

Upper Extremities

Palpation:

Range of Motion:

Motor Exam:

Sensory Exam:

UE Reflexes:

Lower Extremities

Palpation:

Range of Motion:

Motor Exam:

Sensory Exam:

LE Reflexes:

Diagnostic Studies

X-Rays:

MRI:

Photographs:

Depositions:

Records Review:

PREEXISTING RECORDS
CONCLUSIONS

Diagnosis:

Diagnosis Not Related to DOL:

Preexisting Conditions:

Figure 5-1 (continued). Examples of an expert report. (*continued*)

Causation of Diagnosis:

Permanency of Diagnosis:

Physical Limitations in Relationship to Diagnosis:

Medical Necessity of Treatment for Diagnosis:

Medical Billing Review:

Future Medical Treatments in Relationship to Diagnosis:

SUMMATION

Total Time for Preparation of Report: Total time for preparation of this report, including H and P, review of all submitted records and imaging, and dictation of the report, is ____ hours. Opinions are based on the information provided. Any additional information may change my opinions. All opinions are based on a reasonable degree of medical probability.

[Signature Block]

Figure 5-1 (continued). Examples of an expert report.

EXPERT WITNESS REPORT, STATEMENT OF OPINIONS, REASONS, AND BASIS

The first requirement as to a complete **statement of all opinions**, including the reasons and underlying basis, is generally the greatest burden for the expert and is "intended to set forth the substance of the direct examination" of the witness.

COMPLETE STATEMENT

You should consider that the Rule requires a **"complete" report**, which means that you are not permitted to file a preliminary report that is incomplete and then add to the report at a later date. Failure to include all opinions that you intend to testify to may result in the exclusion of those opinions not contained in your report.

The most time-consuming and often most difficult requirement is to provide the basis and reasons for all of your opinions. The Rule and interpreting case law requires that a very detailed and comprehensive discussion of your expert reasoning be provided. Simplistically stated, the court requires you to set forth "how" and "why" the conclusions have been reached and opinions expressed.

In summation, the requirement of an expert report was intended to eliminate unfair surprise to the opposing party and conserve resources. Determination as to the sufficiency of the report has been said to be whether it is sufficiently complete and detailed so that surprise is eliminated, unnecessary depositions are avoided, and costs are reduced.

Expert Witness Report, Other Requirements

The Rule also requires that the expert report contain information considered by the witness in forming the opinions. The use of the term "considered" appears to create a broad disclosure requirement extending beyond information the expert relied on in formulating their opinion. Therefore, any documents reviewed in the course of formulating the opinions should also be disclosed in your report.

Qualifications

The Rule requires the expert witness to set forth their **qualifications**, including a list of any publications authored within the prior 10 years, and should also include the attachment or incorporation of your curriculum vitae.

Compensation

The terms of your retention or payment for testimony are also to be included. This **compensation** may be accomplished by attaching or incorporating your fee agreement with a copy of the report.

List of Other Cases

Finally, the Rule requires a list of any other cases in which you have testified as an expert at trial or deposition within the preceding 4 years. The purpose of this requirement is to enable the adverse party to locate other testimony that you have provided that might be relevant to the present case.

The list should include an identification of the court or agency for which the case was brought, the names of the parties, the case number, and whether the testimony was by deposition or at trial.

Practice Tip

At the outset of your career as a retained expert, you should begin and maintain the appropriate list as required that will save you from frustration and unnecessary countless hours in trying to compile the information from scratch when ordered to do so by the court.

SPOLIATION

It is well settled that a party that reasonably anticipates litigation has an affirmative duty to preserve relevant evidence. Experts, as agents, likewise have a duty to preserve evidence and to exercise reasonable care in the handling of evidence.

Sanctions for spoliation of evidence include a negative inference instruction to the jury, issue preclusion, and outright dismissal of the case.

As a retained expert, you should be cognizant of the effect of destructive testing, that is, where the very test itself may result in destroying a critical item or in rendering further inspection or testing of it useless for purposes of litigation. Such testing should be avoided whenever possible if the opposing party has not been given an opportunity to participate.

Even the fact that the expert may have preserved portions of the relevant items may not be sufficient to avoid sanctions if the court finds that the portions preserved are insufficient for the opposing party to utilize to rebut the expert's opinion. Numerous courts have ordered the exclusion of expert testimony concerning irrelevant item of evidence due to destruction, loss, or alteration of the item, or they have ordered the total exclusion of any evidence concerning the condition of the item. If the plaintiff is the party precluded, such a ruling will often have the effect of preventing them from making a prima facie case; if the defendant is precluded, they may be unable to offer any evidence to rebut the plaintiff's case.

EXPERTS AND TEST EVIDENCE

Often seen in matters involving product liability and/or negligence, testifying experts are often called upon to perform experiments or tests, which are utilized in conjunction with their expert testimony.

For example, a retained expert in the field of biomechanics may conduct a test involving the mechanical movement of crash dummies experienced during a concussion sustained in a football game. The test may have been conducted by the testifying expert or with their assistance or may have been conducted by a third party, such as a government agency or consumer testing group.

With increased availability of more sophisticated forms of technology, the test may be photographed, filmed, videotaped, or, more recently, subject to animation. The resulting product may be offered at trial to be shown to the jury in conjunction with the expert's testimony.

Because this form of experimental or test evidence can have a dramatic impact on the jury, disputes frequently arise as to the circumstances under which such evidence is admissible. Where an experiment or test purports to be a reenactment of an injury or occurrence at issue, it is generally held that the proponent must show that the test was performed under conditions that were substantially similar to those experienced at the time of the injury as to provide a fair comparison between the test and the actual event.

CHAPTER 6

Presentation of Opinions

The essence of our industry is to be able to present something to somebody in the most concise form and in the quickest way possible.

—Maxim Behar

Chapter Objectives

At the completion of this chapter, you will:

- Become familiar with production of opinions through written report or affidavit
- Recognize methods of legal opposition to your written opinions
- Be introduced to oral presentation of opinions through deposition, video recording, or live testimony at trial

Finally, following consultations, review of voluminous records, and examination of the injured party and necessary research, you have come to a conclusion and are ready to present your opinions. How is this accomplished?

Konin JG, Ramey MS. *Becoming an Expert Witness in Health Care and Litigation: A Beginner's Guide* (pp 37-45).
© 2023 SLACK Incorporated.

EXPERT WITNESS REPORT

As discussed in previous chapters, as a testifying expert witness, your opinions and basis for the same will be reduced to writing and provided to the legal counsel retaining your services. Counsel will then disseminate your report to the appropriate parties, pursuant to the Rules of Civil Procedure. Federal Rule of Civil Procedure 26(a)(2)(B) provides that the report is to be "prepared and signed" by the witness (ie, expert). Your report should be written in a manner that reflects your anticipated testimony on the subject. While the majority of the report is written by the expert, review by the retaining attorney is recommended to ensure that all legal questions at issue are encompassed and to ensure that the report satisfies the criteria of the Rule. Prior to finalization, you should allow the attorney to carefully review any report and discuss any matters of concern.

While it is the attorney's responsibility to ensure that the report complies with the Rule, you should ensure that the attorney does not have involvement in the substantive matters except for identification of the medicolegal issues arising in the case. The manner in which the report was drafted will likely be a subject of discovery, and if the expert has simply signed something drafted by the retaining counsel, it will likely be presented to the ultimate fact finder in an effort to undermine your neutrality and credibility.

The deadline for submitting your expert report will generally be controlled by a court's pretrial order. The order typically requires the party having the burden of proof on the issue to submit its expert reports first, with the opposing party having a period of time to submit any reports in rebuttal. Absent a controlling court order, Rule 26(a)(2)(C) specifies that such reports are due no later than 90 days prior to a trial date, except for rebuttal evidence, which is due 30 days after the opponent's disclosures have been made.

AFFIDAVITS AND SUMMARY JUDGMENT

Particularly in cases involving complicated issues of causation and/or liability, a party will likely face a legal challenge as to the sufficiency of evidence in support of their position. In summation, the opposing party will argue to the court that there is insufficient evidence and/or testimony to be relied upon by the trier of fact (ie, judge or jury) in order to decide the matter.

The challenge is typically presented before trial in a motion for summary judgment or during trial on a motion for directed verdict.

Depending upon the party that has retained you, you will likely be required to provide your opinions in an **affidavit** if the issue is raised prior to trial by **motion for summary judgment**. A motion for summary judgment asks the court to issue a final judgment, in this case on the expert's qualifications and opinion. An affidavit is a written statement confirmed by oath and/or affirmation, for use as evidence in court (Figure 6-1). When this occurs, the attorney must determine, in consultation with the expert, the manner in which to draft an affidavit to counter the opponent's motion.

Questions will likely arise as to how much of the information underlying your opinion needs to be set forth in the affidavit and whether foundational documents, such as studies or tests relied on, need to be submitted with the affidavit.

In drafting an affidavit to submit in opposition to a summary judgment motion, you should be aware that the attorney must consider both the sufficiency of your opinion and supporting documentation as well as the admissibility of the affidavit itself.

Your affidavit should initially set forth your qualifications to give an opinion on the subject matter at issue. Except where an expert is obviously unqualified, objections to your qualifications generally go to the weight rather than the admissibility of the affidavit.

The retaining attorney will typically draft an affidavit based upon your written report and/or consultation to comply with the Rules of Evidence. The **Federal Rule of Evidence 705** permits an expert to give an opinion without disclosing the underlying facts or data on which they relied in formulating that opinion, but a party must be careful not to include too little in the affidavit in light of the requirements of the **Federal Rule of Civil Procedure 56(e)**, which requires that affidavits "shall be made on personal knowledge and shall set forth such facts as would be admissible in evidence."

Assuming your expert affidavit contains sufficient information with respect to the facts or data relied upon, the next question is whether the affidavit is subject to attack due to substantive deficiencies in the underlying basis of the opinion. This issue often arises, for example, in tort cases involving conflicting opinions as to whether a plaintiff's symptoms were caused by the traumatic event at issue and may involve an attack on the methodology you have employed as an expert or the reliability of the facts or data you have utilized in formulating your opinions.

AFFIDAVIT OF JOHN SMITH, MD

STATE OF _____

COUNTY OF _____

BEFORE ME, the undersigned authority, personally appeared JOHN SMITH, MD, who, upon oath, stated as follows:

1. I am a medical doctor, specializing in [area]. My curriculum vitae is attached hereto as Exhibit A.

2. I was retained to conduct a Compulsory Medical Examination of [patient name].

3. During my investigation, I reviewed the following items:

    a. [Detailed list of all records reviewed]

    b. [Detailed list of all diagnostic studies reviewed]

4. As part of my investigation, I conducted a physical/neurological examination that consisted of the following:

    a. [Specific examination findings listed here]

5. Based on my education, training, experience, and investigation, it is my opinion within a reasonable degree of medical certainty that:

    a. [Opinion details listed here]

6. I have personal knowledge of the facts set forth herein and, if called to testify to such matters, am competent to do so.

FURTHER AFFIANT SAYETH NAUGHT.

_____

JOHN SMITH, MD

STATE OF _____

COUNTY OF _____

I HEREBY CERTIFY that before me, a Notary Public duly authorized in the State and County named above to administer oaths by means of ☐ Physical Presence **-OR-** ☐ Online Notarization, this _____ day of _____, 2022, by JOHN SMITH, MD, who is ☐ personally known to me **-OR-** ☐ who has produced identification, says that the forgoing affidavit is true and correct.

Type of Identification Produced: _____

_____

Notary Public

_____

Name of Notary Typed, Printed, or Stamped

Place Notary Seal Stamp Above

Figure 6-1. Example of an expert witness written affidavit.

METHODOLOGY

If the methodology utilized is at issue, the court will analyze the reliability of your methodology pursuant to the Federal Rule of Evidence 702. If your affidavit contains a controversial opinion or one that runs counter to the weight of other expert opinions in your field, your opinion will not be rejected for that reason as long as, either in your affidavit itself or other material submitted, the opinion is found to be well reasoned and your methodology acceptable even though your ultimate conclusion may have been at variance with the weight of other expert opinions.

UNDERLYING DATA

If your underlying data are at issue, the court will rely upon the Federal Rule of Evidence 703 to determine whether the facts or data are "of a type reasonably relied upon by experts in the particular field in forming opinions." The proper inquiry is not what the court deems reliable but what the experts in your field of discipline deem to be reliable.

LEGAL STANDARD

In submitting your expert affidavit in opposition to a motion for summary judgment, the attorney should draft your proposed affidavit in terms complying with the correct **legal standard** relevant to the issue under consideration. In most cases, your opinion must be one within a "reasonable possibility" in matters involving product liability and within a "reasonable degree of medical certainty" in matters involving medical testimony. An opinion that is merely "likely" or "possible" is typically deemed insufficient.

DEPOSITIONS AND TRIAL TESTIMONY

The expert **deposition** can often make or break a case. A deposition is the actual process whereby an expert provides a sworn testimony. If a matter is proceeding to a motion for summary judgment and/or trial, a testifying expert should anticipate the scheduling of their deposition for purposes of discovery. Preparation is the key to success.

Quite often, an expert will be inadequately prepared for deposition because they are under the mistaken belief that rigorous preparation is not necessary until trial. This is a significant mistake as every deposition includes both a direct and cross-examination by the opposition. The purpose of the discovery deposition is to aid your opponent in preparation for your cross-examination at trial.

You should be aware that in preparation for this deposition, the experienced opposing counsel will likely be familiar with every fact, document, and witness in the case. They have likely created a medical chronology detailing the subjective complaints and objective findings on examination throughout the injured party's care and treatment, both before and after date of loss. The attorney will likely question you concerning your specific knowledge, or lack thereof, of changes in condition or subsequent intervening events that might contribute to the condition.

The facts of the traumatic incident giving rise to the condition will also be at issue. Inquiry will be made as to your knowledge of these facts and potential mechanism of injury as well as causation. If during deposition you possess insufficient information or knowledge concerning the facts of the event, you can be assured that at trial, the question will arise as to how you have provided an opinion that the injury complained of could be causally related to the event without this knowledge.

During your discovery deposition, by both **direct** and **cross-examination**, inquiry will be made into each of the opinions that you have rendered and explanation as to the specific basis for each.

The attorney retaining you will proceed with a direct examination beginning with the foundation necessary to support your qualifications. Typically, questioning will begin with a recitation of your educational background, training, and professional experience to date. The attorney must establish your expertise within your field of specialty.

The attorney will also establish on the record the materials you have utilized in forming your opinions, as well as methodology and ultimate diagnosis or conclusions that you have made.

Finally, you will be asked to state your opinions within the appropriate standard of proof, that is, "within a reasonable degree of medical certainty" in matters involving medical testimony. Further questioning will involve your opinions concerning the anticipated future need for medical care, restrictions on activities of daily living or employment, and ultimately whether the condition is permanent.

On cross-examination by opposing counsel, you should be aware that the goal is to either (1) undermine your credibility as an expert witness or (2) establish a legal basis to prohibit introduction of your opinion all together.

Typically, questioning on cross-examination will focus on three areas of interest: (1) the experience of the expert to include their background, which allows testimony on the subject; (2) testing and/or methodology to include empirical testing, calculations, and observations; and (3) judgment of the expert, inductive reasoning, or deductive reasoning.

As an expert, you should anticipate that if your opinion is based upon personal experience, counsel will attempt to attack your relative experience, bias, or limitations of experience. If the basis of your opinion is testing, you can anticipate your methodology, test selected, or inferences drawn to be at issue. If the basis of your opinion is your expert judgment, you will be questioned concerning whether reasonable minds can differ depending upon the circumstances.

TRIAL TESTIMONY

Ultimately, a testifying expert will often be called to appear at trial. The secret to successfully presenting an expert in front of a jury is knowing how to "stage" the presentation of that witness's testimony.

The experienced trial attorney will have spent many hours, weeks, or even months in preparation for trial. You should anticipate that the attorneys will have prepared for the direct and cross-examinations of every witness and have knowledge of all anticipated testimony. Through proper pretrial preparation, an experienced attorney will concentrate on their "presentation" of evidence and witnesses for effectiveness at trial before a jury of laypersons.

As an expert testifying witness, you too should be aware that both substance and form matter when presenting your opinions to a judge or jury. The ability to successfully engage a jury will often depend upon both the attorney and expert witness's rapport and style of presentation, use of exhibits, and technique of eliciting opinions and conclusions.

An experienced attorney will attempt to present you to a jury in a way that showcases your capabilities, credibility, and competence. As a testifying expert, you should be prepared and comfortable in front of a jury with an understanding and familiarity with the "stage" on which you will "perform." Prior to your testimony, you should have participated in a pretrial briefing with counsel to discuss your opinions and manner in which questions will be directed. Your pretestimony preparation should also include review of exhibits and/or demonstrative aids that are intended to be used during your testimony. Upon arriving at the courtroom, you should have an opportunity to discuss your testimony with retaining counsel prior to taking the witness stand to obtain information concerning the status of the proceedings and testimony elicited thus far. It would be wise to also familiarize yourself with the courtroom and location of the witness stand, judge, and jury during any break before your call to testify.

Only by being in the courtroom and actually experiencing the various parts of the courtroom setting and being subject to direct and cross-examination in the presence of a jury can you truly appreciate what is involved in the process.

At this final stage of the process, you have fully reasoned and expressed your opinions, have knowledge of all necessary facts in support, and are prepared to provide testimony. Of equal importance to substance is your presentation. Obviously, an expert is anticipated to dress professionally. Upon taking the witness stand, you should have all materials relied upon or necessary to support your testimony, including, if to be used, the proper technology for presentation of exhibits or demonstrative aids. Most important, you should consider your "bedside manner" or ability to communicate effectively with the judge, attorneys, and jury.

The most effective testimony is typically by receiving questions from the attorneys but responding or "talking" to the jury. An effective presentation will involve direct eye contact with the questioning attorney before turning or focusing on the jury when providing answers or certainly explanations of more complex issues. In so doing, you are establishing a rapport with the jurors and enhancing your credibility.

VIDEOTAPING DEPOSITIONS OF EXPERTS FOR USE AT TRIAL

For various reasons, the parties may desire to obtain your opinions and testimony through recording or videotaping your deposition for possible introduction into evidence at trial. One of the primary reasons for doing so is usually to accommodate the busy schedule of a medical expert. Quite often, the medical or health profession's expert will have an ongoing practice and/or clinical responsibility that makes it difficult or inconvenient to be available to testify at trial on a specific date. The scheduling of expert testimony for trial is often complicated by the court's schedule, which may at best narrow the anticipated appearance at trial for the expert to a particular morning or afternoon. It is not unusual for an expert to appear at a certain time but be delayed in testifying due to the status of the court proceedings.

As an alternative, the **Federal Rule of Civil Procedure 30(b)(4)** provides for the taking of depositions by means other than traditional stenographic. With improvements in technology, videotaping of expert depositions has become commonplace and more recently has advanced to virtual appearances through internet platforms such as Zoom and Webex. A decision as to presenting your expert opinion by videotape and/or virtual platform would not only depend on respective scheduling difficulties but also consider the potential disadvantages in doing so. For consideration, live testimony is typically considered more effective than a recording. It allows for not only interaction with the jury and potential to establish a rapport but also flexibility in the ability to respond to evidence and/or testimony received in evidence prior to the expert's appearance. In situations where the expert's testimony has been recorded for use at trial and counsel determines not to call the expert or declines to use the deposition because testimony was not favorable, the opposing party may decide to introduce part or all of the recorded deposition in their own case.

CHAPTER 7

Conflicts of Interest

*Never refuse an assignment except when there is a conflict
of interest, a potential danger to you or your family, or you hold
a strongly biased attitude about the subject under focus.*

—Jessica Savitch

Chapter Objectives

At the completion of this chapter, you will:

- Clearly identify potential conflicts of interest when serving as an expert
- Develop strategies of managing potential and real conflicts of interest
- Establish an ethical foundation behind one's ability to avoid conflicts of interest

Conflicts of interest exist in all walks of life. An expert being asked to provide a professional opinion solely based upon the facts has an obligation to avoid all forms of a conflict of interest. In doing so, the credibility of one's opinion will not be jeopardized by a perceived or real bias.

In its simplest terms, a **conflict of interest** is viewed as a situation in which the concerns or aims of two different parties are incompatible. Additionally, a conflict of interest can also be a situation in which a person is in a position to derive personal benefit from actions or decisions made in their official capacity. When a conflict of interest

Konin JG, Ramey MS. *Becoming an Expert Witness in
Health Care and Litigation: A Beginner's Guide* (pp 47-52).

occurs, an individual becomes unreliable as a result of one's relationship between personal interests and professional obligations.

Generally speaking, existing conflicts of interest may be fairly simple to identify. Others that are perceived to be conflicts may not be so apparent yet can lead to concerns about a named expert providing professional opinions absent a bias foundation. While the American Bar Association and even its Standing Committee on Ethics and Professional Responsibility have established standards that address conflicts of interest for attorneys, conflict of interest rules for experts are virtually nonexistent.

THE LITMUS TEST

As an expert in a health care profession, how do you determine whether or not a conflict of interest exists for a case you have been asked to consider? To begin with, your initial conversation with an attorney or paralegal should involve sharing of certain information to allow you to screen the circumstances.

When an attorney contacts an expert witness, the attorney should provide the following information to the expert witness for conflict check:

- The attorney's name and law firm
- The name(s) of the attorney's client
- The name(s) of the opposing attorney's law firm
- The name(s) of the opposing attorney's party or parties and other individuals and/ or organizations/businesses involved in the case
- The name of the opposing expert witnesses if known at the time

As an invited expert, the first thing you should do is make it aware to the party that contacted you as to whether or not you have a known conflict of interest and, if so, disclose the relationship and in all likelihood respectfully decline your involvement. You should reassess any potential conflicts that you become aware of as you review documents and as the case progresses.

Let's explore some of these initially identified conflicts of interest and provide examples of why immediate disclosure is warranted.

There are truly so many attorneys and law firms that handle personal injury cases that on most occasions, an expert will receive an inquiry from counsel that they have never met before, likely have never heard of, and therefore have no preexisting relationship that would be considered a conflict of interest. However, an expert who performs exemplary work for an attorney and/or firm may be sought after for future work. While this in and of itself is not a conflict of interest, one should be judicious in recognizing when an expert's relationship with an attorney on a repetitive basis will warrant opposing counsel to suggest a biased professional opinion will likely be presented as part of the length and terms of the relationship.

When would multiple scenarios of previous representation of a client or attorney by the same expert be appropriate? Experts within a health care discipline develop specialized areas of knowledge and expertise and will be hired within that scope of practice. Once established, an expert may be hired on multiple occasions to provide an opinion. Likewise, there are attorneys and firms who specialize in certain types of personal injury cases, fraudulent billing, or other health care–related claims. While it makes sense that a single attorney or firm would continue to hire an expert who has proven to deliver a successful outcome for a previous case, let alone multiple cases, this makes for an opposing counsel to raise the concern of a potential conflict of interest based upon the long-lasting relationship and prior engagements.

Recognition of the names of all parties involved is critical to pay early attention to. Generally speaking, a conflict does not exist on the sole reason of name recognition. What is of greater importance is to define the reason for the recognition. For example, if you are simply aware of an opposing client or expert because they are the author of a popular book or article, there is no true perceived conflict. However, if you are asked to defend a client, and you have in fact been a coauthor on several manuscripts with that client, you are clearly in a conflict of interest to defend said client. Similarly, a client for either party may have worked alongside you clinically at one time or another, and you will likely find yourself in a position to defend why an inherent bias would not exist. There are many other examples of conflicts of interest based on the initial recognition of the names of all parties involved. It is up to the expert to inform and disclose all potential known conflicts to counsel as attorneys cannot be expected to know the career paths of each chosen expert. Not doing so would be unethical on the part of an expert and could very possibly damage the case.

Other relationships may exist that should be vetted out before engaging as an expert. It is not uncommon for these to be discovered at some point after an initial formal engagement is made between the expert and the attorney. Here is a list of some examples that may serve as potential conflicts of interest that should be disclosed to one's counsel:

- *Family Members*. In nearly all instances, one would be able to identify if there were a familial relationship from the onset. It is important to mention that knowingly serving as an expert in a case where you represent a family member would immediately raise a bias toward your opinion. It is not likely an attorney or firm would hire you in such case if such a relationship were known. Therefore, again it is your responsibility as an expert to disclose a familial relationship regardless of how close or distant you may be to the client.

- **Colleagues.** In all likelihood, when a colleague is aware of one's experience in serving as an expert, they may lean on them for advice and may encourage the representing counsel to reach out to them for possible engagement. An expert who has a preestablished positive relationship with a current or former colleague will not serve well when it comes to formulating an unbiased professional opinion about the facts of the case. Regardless of the reputation one has of being ethical and professional, the perceived and likely bias will not be seen as impartial to the other parties. Similarly, while you may not be sought out from a current or former colleague who you have not had such a collegial relationship with, if you are asked to serve as an expert for a person who matches this description, in all certainty, the facts of the relationship would eventually be exposed and your service as an expert would be in jeopardy.

- **Competitors.** Any person, company, organization, or other entity for whom you have had an adversarial relationship with would strike you as engaging in expert work against such parties. This may be a person who owns a competing physical therapy practice, a clinical professor or preceptor who did not give you the grade you thought you deserved years ago, or even a competing researcher whose studies and findings you have not agreed with in the past. Any shred of factual or perceived adverse bias will be detrimental to one's case.

- **Former Students.** It might not be uncommon for an expert who has served as a professor, teacher, clinical preceptor, or in other similar mentoring roles to be contacted by former students seeking assistance. While the client may not formally complete an engagement of an expert, one may have knowledge of experts and share with the representing counsel their thoughts. After all, one wants to know the best are being hired in their case. Experts should not be retained by former students in such cases. Neither should an expert agree to engage in a case where a known former student is involved whereby the expert did not previously view this individual favorably. It is important to mention that one who mentors literally thousands of people over the course of a professional career may not recall names of past students immediately. Hence, careful review of all aspects associated with the parties involved is important.

- **Previously Known Knowledge or Communication of the Case.** In some cases, a situation that leads to a claim may have been previously reported in the media. Through social media, views and perspectives may have been shared, including those of the potential expert being considered. An expert being considered for a case must always disclose to the representing counsel any knowledge one has of the case and if they have had any communications with anyone whereby any details of the case have been discussed.

- **Financial Interest.** It should go without saying that an expert who has any past or current financial relationships with any of the parties may have a known conflict of interest. Aside from what we previously discussed as serving as an expert for the same counsel on multiple occasions, other consulting or hired roles should be disclosed. Financial interest from years ago may not qualify as conflicts of interest if all of the parties have changed personnel. Nonetheless, disclosure is always key to avoid raising the issue by surprise.

- **Contractual Relationships With Mutual Parties.** Following an initial screening for conflicts of interest, an expert may come to realize that they have common interests with one of the parties by way of a third or mutual party. This is by no means a reason for stating a conflict of interest upon first learning of the mutual party. It is, however, something that should be disclosed with one's engaged counsel to share the information and be prepared for any tactics used by opposing counsel to claim an established conflict of interest.

- **Future Anticipated Relationships.** When being considered as an expert, not only do existing and past relationships come into play for consideration of potential conflicts of interest, but so do future anticipated circumstances. For example, an expert may be considering, or being considered, to serve in a consulting role with a health clinic or academic health program. The expert would be best served not to engage in a case for or against the party being considered to consult with. In doing so, the expert can simply decline the case and not need to disclose the reasons why. On the other hand, if the expert chooses to consult with the party, they would then be in a known conflict of interest to serve in a legal expert role.

- **Inappropriate Communications During the Case.** Any communications that a retained expert would have during the case with counsel from either party, other witnesses, jurors, or anyone who could influence the expert's opinion could serve as grounds for disqualification for the expert.

PROVING CONFLICT OF INTEREST

If a party believes that a retained expert has a conflict of interest, that party seeking to disqualify the expert has the burden of proof to demonstrate such conflict (Firestone, 2020). Once a party has demonstrated in their opinion that a burden of proof for a conflict of interest is met, the party retaining the expert must prove that no conflict of interest exists to avoid disqualification of the expert.

Aside from the previously mentioned reasons for commonly found conflicts of interest that an expert may be disqualified for, opposing counsels may often times use additional strategies to seek disqualification. Perhaps one becomes aware that the expert has served both counsels in the past at different times in different cases. While some would view this in fact as being fair and impartial, others might move to strike the expert from the case. As most cases do not settle, a record of the expert's testimony may not be found. Cases that are settled, or knowledge gained otherwise, may reveal that the retained expert was previously disqualified in another case due to a conflict of interest, whereby counsel may move to demonstrate a pattern-like behavior and a potential risk to allow the expert to establish credibility in the current case.

THE TEST FOR INDEPENDENCE

With minimal standards in place to define a conflict of interest from a straightforward perspective, how does one determine what is an absolute or perceived conflict of interest? The *Protocol for the Instruction of Experts to Give Evidence in Civil Claims* describes a method by which a potential expert can view a conflict of interest in a civil case. Simply put, would an expert express the same opinion if given the same instructions by another party? This in and of itself does not rule out any conflict of interest. However, experts should not place themselves in a position to promote or endorse an opinion because it is in agreement with, or because they are being instructed by, the party they have engaged with. In other words, the duty of an expert is to provide an unbiased opinion based upon the facts of a case and not to serve the exclusive interest of the party who they are retained by. An expert is not an advocate despite being hired by counsel who likely feels their opinion is in support of one's client.

Some final tips to keep in mind as an expert to avoid engaging in a case where a known or potential conflict of interest would lead to a disqualification:

- Always declare known or potential conflicts of interest as soon as possible.
- Stay informed and disclose any new potential conflicts of interest that may arise while you have been retained as an expert.
- Maintain your confidentiality at all times and do not disclose confidential information that becomes a conflict of interest.
- Maintain impartiality at all times with your opinion as an expert.
- Create a checklist for each potential engagement to review any conflicts of interest.

CHAPTER 8

Establishing a Fee Structure

Money is only a tool. It will take you wherever you wish,
but it will not replace you as the driver.

—Ayn Rand

Chapter Objectives

At the completion of this chapter, you will:
- Identify key components of an expert's fee structure
- Assess the importance of an engagement letter
- Establish your own value and develop an expert fee structure

Providing expert services at a professional level is in fact a job. While it may not be a vocation by trade per se, it is in fact a role that not all professionals can qualify for. Therefore, it is totally acceptable to be reasonably compensated for one's time, effort, and expertise. For someone starting out in their first case as an expert, establishing rates for one's fees may be one of the most difficult steps to take. Where do you start? First and foremost, seek advice from others you know and trust. Fees for expert services are not readily advertised and promoted in the public domain. You can search cyberspace but will likely come up empty handed. You also must learn what is considered reasonable and fair for your particular discipline.

Konin JG, Ramey MS. *Becoming an Expert Witness in Health Care and Litigation: A Beginner's Guide* (pp 53-64).
© 2023 SLACK Incorporated.

Simply throwing out a number when you are contacted to serve as an expert is not a smart solution. You will be expected to confidently provide your fees, in writing, and rather quickly. The document that you provide is referred to as a **fee structure**. A fee structure is a representation of the various services that you will provide as an expert and the remuneration requested for each. The thought process is fairly simple and involves three easy steps as a guide. Given your level of expertise and experience, answer the following questions:

1. What dollar amount do you value your time and expertise without pricing yourself out of an expert role?
2. What dollar amount is equitable for your time and expertise without undervaluing your worth?
3. What is considered by others with knowledge to be the general going rate for an expert's fees?

Over time, and with experience and feedback, an expert becomes much more knowledgeable and comfortable in establishing a fee schedule for the various types of work one can perform. Until then, where do you start besides gathering general intelligence as aforementioned? Some look at their current circumstances, either as a clinician or as an academic, and use their hourly wages in those settings as a template. In other words, if you make $100/hour in a clinical setting treating a patient, then that is your value and you can justify such a fee. The truth is, using your day job wages as a metric is a faulty approach. While you might be considered an expert at what you do clinically or academically, conveying such expertise when retained for a lawsuit requires an additional skill set and time away from your regular job or obligations. Therefore, your rates should be higher in general, and you will want to spend considerable time preparing a fee structure that is pleasing to the party hiring you for your services and likewise respectable of your time and expertise.

In essence, the fee structure is a menu of all of your services that you are asking to be paid by the party seeking to hire you as an expert. All fee structures will be reviewed, in addition to your credentials and experience, prior to anyone being contractually obligated. In addition to your direct content knowledge, additional considerations are included in fees that you may want to charge for during the process of serving as a retained expert.

PREPARING A FEE SCHEDULE

As previously mentioned, one's expert fee schedule should be carefully thought out. Multiple categories should be included in an effort to provide the hiring party with a comprehensive awareness of your expectations to be paid for your work (Figure 8-1). The most common categories provided in a fee structure include:

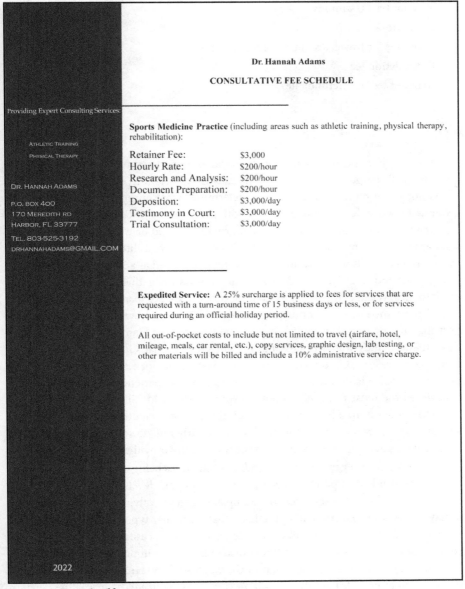

Dr. Hannah Adams

CONSULTATIVE FEE SCHEDULE

Providing Expert Consulting Services:

ATHLETIC TRAINING

PHYSICAL THERAPY

DR. HANNAH ADAMS

P.O. BOX 400

170 MEREDITH RD

HARBOR, FL 33777

TEL. 803-525-3192

DRHANNAHADAMS@GMAIL.COM

Sports Medicine Practice (including areas such as athletic training, physical therapy, rehabilitation):

Retainer Fee:	$3,000
Hourly Rate:	$200/hour
Research and Analysis:	$200/hour
Document Preparation:	$200/hour
Deposition:	$3,000/day
Testimony in Court:	$3,000/day
Trial Consultation:	$3,000/day

Expedited Service: A 25% surcharge is applied to fees for services that are requested with a turn-around time of 15 business days or less, or for services required during an official holiday period.

All out-of-pocket costs to include but not limited to travel (airfare, hotel, mileage, meals, car rental, etc.), copy services, graphic design, lab testing, or other materials will be billed and include a 10% administrative service charge.

2022

Figure 8-1. Example of fee structure.

- Hourly rates
- Purchasing and copying costs
- Postage and shipping fees
- Rate for deposition

- Rate for trial testimony
- Pro bono work
- Expenses for travel, accommodations, and meals
- Cancellation fee
- Retainer fee (nonrefundable)

Hourly Rates

The simplest and most common question an expert receives upon an inquiry is what one will charge as an hourly rate. It really is important to emphasize that a number is not just a number, and how one determines what an hourly rate is should be grounded in considerable thought along with the ability to justify one's rates.

The first step in determining one's hourly rate should be a search of the industry standards. This is not easily found online, yet may require as little as a few phone calls to experienced colleagues willing to share their knowledge and attorneys willing to offer honest and sound advice. Based on the information gathered, one would benchmark themselves in comparison to existing expert fees. For example, if an expert who has been retained in 25 previous cases charges $500/hour, how would a first-time expert align their fees relative to the limited case experience? Many might suggest that in this situation, one's hourly rate should be much less, perhaps in the $250/hour range. However, there are additional circumstances to consider. For example, what if the area of one's expertise is unique, and despite limited past experience as an expert, one is considered the most prominent known expert in the field? Should that value translate into a request for a higher hourly rate? There is no absolute answer here. What is absolute is that anyone wishing to establish an hourly rate do some homework on the industry rates and expert credentials of those currently providing expert services.

Once you have a general understanding of the rates being offered in the industry, it would be prudent to perform a self-assessment of your level of expertise. This may or may not be discipline specific. For example, in cases involving a physical therapist, it may be best to be licensed and practicing that particular type of physical therapy to serve as a credible witness. In other situations, it may be a case such as a sport-related concussion, which could cross multiple disciplines based upon the type of expertise needed in the case. Was the concern how the concussion was managed on the field? In this case, an athletic trainer or physician expert may be needed. Or was the concern based on the rehabilitation that may have occurred within physical or occupational therapy? What is your particular expertise? Ask yourself the following questions:

- How many years have you been in practice as a professional?
- Do you have evidence of peer-reviewed original research and/or professional presentations on the content of expertise?

- Have you received awards or recognition for your work on the content?
- Do you hold leadership positions within your professional organization?
- Have you led committees or task forces on the subject area?
- Have you developed tools, products, and so on that have assisted in the management of the content?
- Do you have experience consulting in the content area?
- Do you have any previous experience being retained as an expert?
- Have you previously written affidavits, given depositions, or testified in court?

You may receive additional advice from trusted sources that will provide additional considerations for how you should establish your hourly rate. For example, many experts have set a variable hourly fee structure based upon what types of services are being performed. Different types of work performed by the hour may include reviewing medical records, performing research, preparing documents, and performing peer review. You may charge a flat hourly fee for each of these types of services, or you may distinguish among each and assign different hourly rates. Some experts also perform what is called **peer review**, a process whereby a primary expert may have been retained, and a secondary expert is hired simply to review the primary expert's findings, such as what is written in an affidavit. Experts may charge a slightly less hourly rate as a peer reviewer as they do not have as much involvement in the case. On the other hand, peer reviews oftentimes require a relatively quick turnaround of opinion, and therefore some experts may not charge any less of a fee for this service.

An expert should view one's time regardless of how it is being assigned toward work for a case. For example, time spent on telephone calls, online video meetings, and other methods of tasks required to fulfill one's obligations as an expert in a case should also be recorded.

Clearly not all work performed occurs in hourly increments. Therefore, one should establish a clear fee structure. In doing so, terms should be defined in 15-, 30-, or 45-minute increments and how rounding off is determined. This will avoid any discrepancies and disagreement when it comes time to provide an invoice for services performed. All hourly work should be tracked in terms of the amount of time work is performed and on what day. It is reasonable to provide updates to the hiring firm specifically as your hours increase during a case.

One last consideration related to one's hourly rate is when a response is requested by counsel for an expert in a timeline that is considered to be expeditious and not within reason of one's normally needed time to review documents and/or provide verbal or written feedback. In such cases, and made clear in the expert's **engagement letter**, a surcharge can be applied for the services provided. An engagement letter is a contractual written document between the expert and the retaining counsel that outlines the responsibilities of each party (Figure 8-2).

December 15, 2020

Kyle Nujax, Esquire
Law Office of Kyle Nujax
205 E. Dom Ave.
Somerset, MA 44502

Dear Mr. Nujax,

Thank you for contacting me regarding your need for an expert to review matters related to the Gina Maldoffio case. Your confidence in my ability to assist you in this matter is greatly appreciated.

Before I begin work on this matter, please review my fee schedule and payment policies, which shall be in effect for the duration of our work on this case:

1. Services rendered, including file review, research and analysis, site inspections, meetings, phone conferences, written and electronic correspondence, report writing, and travel will be invoiced at a rate of $200 per hour.

2. Trial and deposition testimony will be invoiced at a rate of $3,000 per day or partial day of testimony. Payment for these services must be received in full prior to appearance. I reserve the right to cancel a trial or deposition appearance for nonpayment.

3. Cancellation of an appearance for trial or deposition with less than 48 hours notice will result in a $1,000 cancellation fee, plus the cost of any nonrefundable travel expenses.

4. All out-of-pocket costs to include but not limited to travel (airfare, hotel, mileage, meals, car rental, etc.), copy services, graphic design, lab testing, or other materials will be billed to you and will include a 10% administrative service charge.

5. Invoices will be prepared on a regular basis while work is in progress and at the completion of requested work. Payment of invoices is due upon receipt. After 30 days, balances will accrue a 1.5% interest penalty per month. I reserve the right to discontinue work at any time for non-payment of outstanding invoices.

6. This agreement is strictly between the law office of Kyle Nujax and Dr. Hannah Adams. Therefore, you are directly responsible for payment of all invoices.

7. Expedited Services: Any work requested with a turn-around time of 15 business days or less or any work required during an official holiday period will be subject to a 10% administrative surcharge.

8. Engagement for Services: In order to secure my services, an engagement fee of $3,000 is required. This fee is considered forward payment for services and will be applied to the first invoice. This engagement fee is nonrefundable in any event.

If you understand and agree to the terms described in this letter, please sign below and return this letter with the $3,000 engagement fee payable to Dr. Hannah Adams. Receipt of this signed agreement and engagement fee signifies your understanding and agreement with the terms described in this letter and guarantees exclusive availability of my services for your case. Please note, I am not retained, and you may not identify me as your expert in this case until I have received back your signed copy of this letter, together with the full payment of the engagement fee. I look forward to working with you on this case. Please forward all case materials in care of: Dr. Hannah Adams, PO Box 400, 170 Meredith Road, Harbor, FL 33777. Please also inform me prior to any mailings so that I can confirm a timely receipt.

If you have any questions, please do not hesitate to call.

Very Truly Yours,

Accepted and Agreed:

Dr. Hannah Adams   Law Office of Kyle Nujax

Hannah Adams, PhD

By:_____ Print Name:_____
Date:_____

Providing Expert Consulting Services:

ATHLETIC TRAINING
PHYSICAL THERAPY

DR. HANNAH ADAMS

P.O. BOX 400
170 MEREDITH RD
HARBOR, FL 33777
TEL. 803-525-3192
DRHANNAHADAMS@GMAIL.COM

2022

Figure 8-2. Example of an expert's engagement letter with a lawyer.

Purchasing and Copying Costs

As part of one's expert work, one may need to pay for access to necessary materials deemed relevant to a case and/or make copies of materials or exhibits to be used for deposition or testimony. These expenses do not fall under an hourly wage category. If an expert expects the hiring firm to absorb these costs, it will need to be stated so in the fee schedule provided or in one's engagement letter.

Postage and Shipping Fees

Experts may also encounter situations whereby they will receive or send packages of materials of all different sizes as part of the case. In some instances, documents pertaining to the case could come in as many as 3 to 5 large boxes and be expected to be returned to the hiring firm upon the completion of the case. Again, any fees incurred by the expert related to postage and shipping should be delineated in the fee structure or engagement letter as to the expectations of whose responsibility it is to cover these costs.

Rate for Deposition

Participating in a deposition as an expert necessitates a different approach toward remuneration for one's time. Instead of billing using an hourly rate, depositions often times yield a flat rate charged by the half or full day of one's time. Some experts may go as far as requesting a minimum fee for a deposition appearance, typically 3 to 4 hours, which would qualify for the half-day rate. It is wise for an expert to require the retaining counsel be billed for deposition fees. Experienced experts require payment in advance when being deposed by the opposing counsel. The reason for this is unfortunately a pattern of failure to receive payment from opposing counsels. In the case where the time of the deposition exceeds the amount of prepayment, experts will typically continue with the deposition and bill the remainder. This is done at the risk of not receiving final additional payments. The alternative is to not continue with the deposition until receiving additional payment at that time. This can make for an awkward situation that most experts would prefer to avoid. The key is to clarify your terms in the engagement letter.

Rate for Trial Testimony

"Trial testimony" is really a term that describes all aspects of an expert's involvement when a case goes to trial. Setting fees for a trial is in many ways similar to that of a deposition in that most experts prefer to bill by the half or full day vs using an hourly rate. To begin with, an expert may be brought in to actually testify in a trial, but that is not the case at all times. Sometimes, testimony is not necessary, but the hiring counsel chooses to have the expert present for assistance of any kind that may be needed.

Fees that may also be included under the umbrella of trial testimony include basic attendance and presence, meetings with counsel, advice and suggestions provided to counsel regarding cross-examination, and planning for direct examination.

Pro Bono Work

While not something seen all that often, some experts will agree to work on a case pro bono. As a relatively new expert, one benefit of working pro bono is that quality work delivered for a client may lead to future paid work or other opportunities found to be helpful when one is building an expert business.

Expenses for Travel, Accommodations, and Meals

Expenses associated with travel, accommodations, and meals usually pertain to that of a trial or required deposition to be given at a location distant to the expert's home. Travel time, as well as specific requests/needs for accommodations and meals, should be addressed clearly in one's engagement letter. In addition, how such expenses will be paid and who will be responsible for making such arrangements should also be agreed upon in advance.

With respect to travel time, some experts expect to be paid at their standard hourly rate. Other experts will bill a flat fee per half or full day of travel. The logic behind being paid during travel is that an expert is applying their personal time toward a particular case. Additionally, since the travel time may include working, such as reading materials and/or accessible use of a laptop computer, some experts will require first-class airfare purchases for planes and trains. Experienced experts may request specific accommodations such as certain hotel chains and rooms that have office-type suites available to work in.

Travel by personal vehicle is not uncommon for short trips and is equitably reimbursed to the expert using the federal government mileage rates. Meal per diems can also be reimbursed using the government rates. Again, the specific terms should be clarified in the engagement letter, especially if an expert wishes to request higher rates for meals.

Cancellation Fee

Experts learn that the legal system can be an untimely and unpredictable endeavor. Perhaps one of the most frustrating experiences is having a scheduled deposition or trial cancelled or postponed to a future date for consideration. For this reason, it is prudent to build into one's fee schedule a cancellation fee. This is justified given the fact that the expert has blocked away valuable time dedicated to a particular case and will be unable to reschedule other work upon an unplanned cancellation. A reasonable cancellation fee can include all or part of the standard deposition or trial fees that have been agreed upon. When establishing a cancellation fee, a time clause should be considered in an effort to be fair to all parties. Most would agree that 48 hours is fair notice for a cancellation to avoid any cancellation fees. For clinicians, this will likely be enough time to reschedule patients. For academicians, a 2-day notice should work well with planned coursework. This is another reason why some experts choose to ensure deposition and trial fees are paid in advance as it may not be as easy to collect a cancellation fee.

Retainer Fee

A **retainer fee** is a form of a deposit provided to the expert in good faith as part of being retained and accepting the engagement terms. The majority of experts, regardless of discipline, will obtain some sort of retainer prior to performing any work for a client. The amount retained varies from person to person, with minimum retainers found in the ballpark of $1,500 and higher-end retainers requested at $5,000 and up. Some have suggested using higher retainers when engaging with insurance companies in a defense case as collecting fees can become a challenge secondary to the bureaucracy of the process. If a case goes to trial, a judge may ask for an expert to justify one's fees, so always be prepared to defend the numbers and how they were derived.

A retainer also serves as a safety net for an expert to ensure initial payment. One form of a commonly used retainer is referred to as **replenishable.** With a replenishable retainer, the expert deducts billable hours from the fees that have already been paid in the retainer. If a replenishable retainer is exhausted, the billable rates in accordance with the **engagement letter** and fee schedule would then be applied.

Engagement letters should specify the type of retainer being used. For example, with a replenishable retainer, if a case settles prior to the expert providing billable hours equal to the amount of the retainer, the expert may be required to reimburse the client for unused fees. Therefore, the engagement letter should describe whether the retainer is in fact partially refundable or nonrefundable. Given these terms, the expert and the client should agree on a reasonable retainer that estimates the amount of initial work that may be needed by the expert to perform.

Engagement letters come in all forms and are specific to the expert's preference. Some other considerations to include in an engagement letter to clarify the terms of an agreement may also include the fact that the retaining counsel is responsible for fee payments, not the lawyer's client. Though it may not be easy to enforce, some stipulate charging interest for fees not paid by the requested dates set forth in a contract.

INVOICE FOR BILLABLE WORK

All experts should meticulously keep track of the time spent applied toward work with a retained case. This should include not only the amount of time worked but also specifically what type of work is being billed for each time. For example, is a billable hour related to a call with an attorney, reading witness depositions, or any other required activity for the case? Additionally, an expert should maintain a running tabulation of the total number of billable hours at each rate and the total running cost to the client. It is fair to inform the client when a retainer has been or is close to being met. It is also fair to send monthly statements to the client for the purposes of open and honest communications. All too often, experts will report difficulties in getting paid, including from the retaining counsel. The more one is organized and communicable, the less likely surprises may occur (Figure 8-3).

ETHICAL PRACTICES FOR EXPERT BILLING

Serving as an expert certainly requires a professional level of competence in order to effectively perform the role. Additionally, as a result of the risk assumed relative to one's own personal reputation and liability, as well as the exchange of fees for services, an expert must understand the ethical aspect of the business component as it relates to billing practices. Operating in an ethical manner should be no surprise to a professional who has most likely upheld such standards over their entire career. More than likely, any questionable ethics related to serving as an expert will arise from one simply not being informed of what is considered to be an unethical decision or way of managing one's business side of being an expert.

Experts are oftentimes advised to establish a limited liability corporation (LLC) or some other entity as a way of protecting their personal assets and also more efficiently tracking their expenses and revenues related solely to their expert work. When a business is established, it may include promotional and marketing materials (brochures, websites, social media) designed to inform potential clients of one's expert services. All forms of information dissemination in these examples must remain impartial to avoid demonstrated conflict of interest partisan views.

INVOICE

P.O. Box 1422
Safety Harbor, FL 34695
Tel. 888-444-8754

INVOICE NO.	19OH65472-02
DATE	March 16, 2022
CUSTOMER ID	19OH6547

TO　Mr. Marshall Sykes
8809 Smithtown Road
Suite A
Hamden, CT 06514

Consultant	Your File No.	Matter	Payment Terms
Konin	OH45678	Frederick Jones v. State of Connecticut	On Receipt

Date	DESCRIPTION	Hours	Rate	Total
3/17/2022	Initial Retainer			$ (5,000.00)
4/1/2022	Client Telephone Consultation	0.50	495.00	$ 247.50
4/1/2022	File Review: Bergmeir & Ludwig Depositions	3.00	495.00	$ 1,485.00
4/4/2022	File Review: Stanly & Angst Depositions	3.00	495.00	$ 1,485.00
4/5/2022	File Review: McCullough & White Depositions	2.00	495.00	$ 990.00
4/6/2022	File Review: Osborne & Miller Depositions	2.50	495.00	$ 1,237.50
4/7/2022	Document Preparation	2.00	495.00	$ 990.00
4/8/2022	Document Preparation	4.00	495.00	$ 1,980.00
4/12/2022	Peer Review	2.00	495.00	$ 990.00
4/15/2022	Replenishable Retainer (Refundable per agreement)			$ 10,000.00
				$ -
				$ -
				$ -
				$ -
				$ -
				$ -
				$ -
				$ -
				$ -
				$ -
			SUBTOTAL	$ 14,405.00
			TOTAL	$ 14,405.00

Make all checks payable to The Rehberg Konin Group, LLC

THANK YOU FOR YOUR BUSINESS!

Figure 8-3. Example of an expert billing invoice.

Expert contracts should be developed with independent legal advice to not only protect the expert in a binding agreement but also ensure fairness to the retaining client. Serving as an expert is never about "winning" a contract—it is about providing a service at an equitable rate absent partial views and biases.

Therefore, as previously stated, compensation for expert services should be fair, reasonable, and commensurate with one's level of expertise and the time and effort involved. Experts should be cautious to not enter into contracts in which the fees for one's services are disproportionately high relative to one's expertise and the time and effort involved. Furthermore, an expert should never enter into a contract where the fees for one's services are contingent upon the outcome of the case.

Closing Thoughts to Consider

An expert is essentially a consultant, and when money is exchanged, it becomes a consulting business. Health care experts are not always adequately prepared to operate in a business consulting role and must learn the nuances associated with best practices. These include all ethical, legal, financial, and other related possibilities. Furthermore, it is likely for most that serving in an expert consulting role with a formal contractual and business relationship could in fact be considered a conflict of interest with one's primary employer. Ensuring and avoiding outside activity conflicts should be managed prior to engaging into binding contracts.

Avoiding primary employment conflicts of interest with outside activity such as expert consulting also requires careful use of one's time and equipment. For example, all expert work should be performed using one's personal (or consulting business) computer, laptop, cellphone, printer, and so on. Using one's primary employer's equipment can only be done if such permission is granted when disclosing outside activity. Otherwise, even with approval for outside activity, using the employer's equipment could pose a conflict. It goes without saying that consulting work should not occur on one's primary employer's time either unless approved to do so.

With that being said, an expert consult will incur costs that may not oftentimes be thought of when beginning a consulting business as an expert. One should plan to absorb the costs of not only computer hardware and accessories but also other necessities, such as wireless services, office space, a separate professional liability insurance plan, billing software, and possibly a post office box to keep professional correspondence distinct from one's personal residence.

CHAPTER 9

Expert Promotion

When it comes to content, the best marketers know that self-promotion is good.

—Kieran Flanagan

Chapter Objectives

At the completion of this chapter, you will:

- Learn how to effectively market your expert legal services
- Identify appropriate expert characteristics to possess and market
- Recognize approaches that are not ideal for expert marketing

As an individual interested in putting one's professional expertise to work in the legal world, one must find a way, or multiple ways, of getting on the radar of those retaining the experts. After all, you may be one of the sole recognized experts in your field, but you still need to have methods for lawyers, paralegals, insurance companies, and others to find you and learn of your capabilities. This chapter will offer suggestions as to how one can effectively market expert legal services.

Konin JG, Ramey MS. *Becoming an Expert Witness in Health Care and Litigation: A Beginner's Guide* (pp 65-73).

What Is Marketing?

In its simplest terms, marketing is an action or process of promoting and/or selling one's product or services. In the case of an expert, the product is one's service. According to the American Marketing Association, marketing also includes a process for communicating, delivering, and exchanging offerings that have value for customers, clients, partners, and society at large. It all begins, however, with first and foremost knowing exactly what your expertise is and to ensure you strategically develop your brand so that it is not necessarily you but rather others who perceive you to be an expert. "Others" may consist of professional colleagues and peers. This may be based on your professional accomplishments that they are privy to, such as publications, presentations, or sitting alongside you on a committee. In these cases, individuals simply through word of mouth will share over time their thoughts in the professional community through both formal and casual conversation of your perceived expertise. The key with intentional marketing is to ensure that those who will do the actual hiring have knowledge of your expert reputation and then your ultimate service delivery model. To achieve such visibility and status, one needs to establish a brand or a reputation of excellence as an expert in a chosen area. A brand associates an expert with a specific skill set and serves to differentiate one from another.

One's ability to inform others, also referred to as networking, remains a powerful and beneficial tool in advancing expert opportunities. Strategically identifying events to have a presence at increases one's exposure and opportunities to meet others, including attorneys. This may require thinking slightly differently in that you would search for legal conferences in your area or even on a national scale vs attending only your typical health care and profession-specific annual meetings and conferences. In some cases, acquiring membership in associations can provide you the necessary information of where and when conferences will be held and may also afford you a membership discount to attend. On a local basis, you can find everything from luncheon gatherings to weekend mini-courses that will minimize your overall expenses and invested travel time. Regardless of the event you attend, always be prepared to give your "elevator pitch" in 30 seconds or less upon introductions to potential clients. Also, be ready for the common basic types of questions you may receive as others inquire of your expertise: what areas are you an expert, how many cases you have done, who you have represented, and so on. Once you become familiar with a type of conference, you may opt to submit proposals to more actively participate, such as in giving a formal presentation. This serves as an excellent opportunity for you to not only promote yourself in general but also convey your grasp and familiarity with content knowledge and your professional appearance and communication skills. These are the types of presentations you should be on your highest "A-game" with respect to rehearsal and delivery.

Prior to determining how one will choose to market as an expert, it is vitally impor-tant to understand what qualities are viewed as contributing to an expert portfolio that potential clients will look for. As each of these is identified, the expert should ensure that they are addressed as best as possible prior to making available for public viewing. Let's discuss some of these important elements that make up an effective expert's brand.

Experience

Without a doubt, possessing firsthand experience in the content matter is essen-tial. If the area is clinically related, it certainly adds to the credibility of an expert to actively be engaged in clinical practice. Individuals can continue to serve as an expert soon after no longer being involved with clinical practice, though expertise may be challenged if too much time has passed as a result of discontinuing clinical practice. While there is not a set time frame, a couple of years after clinical practice may tend to raise questions. With that said, one may be out of clinical practice but asked to serve as an expert for a case where the alleged injury claim occurred 18 months ago while one was still actively practicing. This should not prevent one from serving as an expert. Furthermore, while discontinuing clinical practice, someone who remains actively in-volved with consulting, research, and/or administrative aspects of the clinical skills would more than likely still qualify as an expert. It becomes an additional concern when an individual is no longer involved with active clinical practice or any other form of demonstrated professional engagement other than serving in the role of a so-called professional expert. This will more than likely be challenged by opposing counsel as one seeking a means of additional revenue and for no other purpose.

Clinical Practice

With respect to overall experience, both as it relates to clinical practice and other areas of one's expertise, it should be clearly, consistently, and accurately detailed in all publications, presentations, and other avenues of publicly found information. Some experts are very specialized and are recognized in a singular area of expertise, making it very easy to promote the relationship one has to their professional identification. On the other hand, some experts are involved in content that enables one to possess expertise in a variety of areas. While this is possible, expert promotion should always be careful not to spread one too thin as in serving as a jack-of-all-trades. Doing so may not be believable, may prevent one from being retained, or may lead to a less-than-desirable experience when challenged by opposing counsel and experts. In the health care field, many examples of this exist. One may possess expert content knowledge in such areas as sport concussion. Yet, the variety of expertise may very well differentiate an expert's status. For example, an individual may be involved in basic science research and published dozens of articles on the chemical changes that the brain undergoes following a sport concussion. However, if this expert were to testify, they may be challenged on their actual clinical practices in dealing with concussions when they actually happen on the sidelines or participating in the rehabilitation process. On the contrary, a very experienced clinician who regularly evaluates and treats individuals with sport concussions may be not as adept at reciting the basic science knowledge as reported in the literature in as much detail as the first expert could. Keep in mind that expertise would also be required as it relates to the standard of care, so regardless of one's basic science or clinical practice, background testimony would require an expert's opinion as to the adherence of following the standard of care for the overall management of sport concussion.

Educational Background

The formal educational training of an expert will be analyzed and should serve as an overall strength for one to market and promote. This begins with one's completed academic degrees. The educational institution, the reputation of the school, and degree area that one studied can be helpful to lay an early foundation of formal training to market one's lengthy and successful professional career. Individuals who possess advanced training or credentials should showcase such achievements. While promoting advanced training, it is also imperative to not exaggerate the nature of the knowledge gained. Experts should carefully judge the authenticity and credibility of any certification, certificate, or other additional educational accomplishment to be certain that it is truly recognized as a reputable program. Promoting credentials and "letters" after one's name that have questionable character related to their organization or quality of content delivered will raise challenges for an expert to defend on deposition or testimony and run the risk of an individual's own expertise being in question.

Medicolegal Experience

The ability to claim past experience as an expert is a plus and should be used as a strength for an expert to seek further retainment in cases. While there may be many individuals in different health care fields who possess specific content knowledge expertise, not the same can be said for many of these same persons possessing familiarity with the medicolegal process. Retaining parties much prefer an expert with previous experience. Upon initial contact, in addition to requesting one's fee schedule and any potential conflicts of interest, an expert will be asked about previous experience with the medicolegal system. This will include details about which cases and if and how often one has been deposed and testified in court. Experts should maintain a spreadsheet of past experiences as a resource to demonstrate preparedness for future inquiries. Additionally, references related to each of those cases may be requested and can be provided in the document. This would not be made publicly available but instead used only upon request (Table 9-1).

Table 9-1

EXAMPLE OF SPREADSHEET OF PAST EXPERT EXPERIENCES

Case	Retained By	Role	Contribution	Result	Contact Info
Helen Smith v. Mountain Physical Therapy Clinic, LLC	Plaintiff	Expert	Affidavit, deposition	Settled	Steven L. Joseph Law Office of Bunnell & Taylor 87 Pine Needle Drive Dallas, TX 75116
Nikita Hedman v. State of Florida	Plaintiff	Expert	Affidavit, deposition	Settled	Margo Lowry Law Offices of Margo Lowry 6565 Giganto Lane Tallahassee, FL 32309
Daniel & Mary Hightower, on behalf of Rebecca Hightower v. Elite University	Defense	Expert	Affidavit, deposition, testimony	Trial	Lori Menuchin Monroe & Monroe, P.A. 4100 Tower Circle New York, NY 10024
Thomas Cornwall v. East County Public School District	Plaintiff	Expert, consultant	Data collection	Settled	Elliott Spencer The Rubenstein Firm 11456 Argyle Road Atlanta, GA 30304
Laruen Batts v. Sports Medicine Services of Atlanta, LLC	Defense	Expert	Affidavit	Settled	Scott L. Weinstein Weinstein & Horowitz, P.A. 100 East Typhoon Drive Clearwater, FL 33759

When referring to past experience, there are a number of important items that an expert is familiar with that a first-time expert would lack experience with. In fact, the very reason this book exists is to assist the content expert but novice legal expert with the basic tools to become more competent in the system. An experienced expert is more likely to extrapolate the standards of care for a case and provide an opinion based on the type of proof necessary to meet for each case. An experienced expert will have quality written reports in a format and language that demonstrates one's grasp of the task as an expert. Likewise, being able to convey one's expert opinion verbally, either through deposition or testimony, is essential. Being present, or nowadays even via videotape, for a cross-examination by an opposing counsel is not an episode one may like to have all too often. It can be unpleasant at times, and the ability to maintain one's composure and still serve as a credible expert is something even the best of the best experts will struggle with at times.

Demeanor and Communications Skills

It should come as no surprise that the role of an expert requires the highest level of professionalism. A content expert entering the medicolegal world must be able to not only clearly articulate well with all parties, including potential juries, but must do so in a manner that is composed, exudes confidence yet not arrogance, and comes across overall as convincing and unbiased. A major responsibility of an expert is to articulate complex issues to all counsel and jury members. This is typically done by transferring scientific terminology into layperson's terms while still upholding the strongest of evidence to support one's professional opinion. A very common tactic for opposing counsel is to disrupt the calm and assuring composure of an expert. This can be done by meticulously critiquing an expert's résumé for errors, omissions, and even the ever-so-slightly misguided adjective. The objective of opposing counsel is to change the otherwise calm behavior of an expert to one of discomfort, uncertainty, and even anger. Though knowing what to expect and properly preparing for such cross-examinations, even the most seasoned expert at times will reach a point of inability to brush off the aggressive questioning of a skilled attorney. An expert who seeks additional work should be sure to polish one's professional demeanor for the medicolegal system equally as much as one's content knowledge of a case.

How to Find Experts

Finding an expert for cases is not always an easy task. It can be somewhat time consuming, and it may not be facilitated by the best approach at all times. The more specific the expertise required, the more difficult it may be at times to find the right expert. There are some tried-and-true methods that have been proven to work, and there are still firms that assign a paralegal to "google" key terms. Personal injury firms that have found success using a certain expert may prefer to keep that individual on file for future cases. On some occasions, firms who have opposed an expert but have been impressed with the expert overall have retained that individual for a future case. Sometimes, calls placed to colleagues can yield a referral that works out well. For these reasons, many consider repeat business and referrals the gold standard for expert marketing. Because of the lengthy time that it takes to identify the right expert, attorneys will rely on expert witness service directories that shoulder much of the load of screening experts. As a new expert seeking professional opportunities in the medicolegal system, it is beneficial to learn the common practices that attorneys seek to find you.

All materials should always be carefully proofread prior to disseminating. It is imperative to have extra sets of eyes on your résumé, website, engagement letters, and all else. If you use a website, keep it simple yet comprehensive without errors. Your materials and public presence should brand you in a professional manner without the glitter of too much promotion. In essence, you want to make yourself known and available, but you do not want to come across as if you are selling services in a desperate manner. This is referred to as a hired gun, and it can backfire against you in that the opposing counsel may try to portray you as an expert who will say whatever is necessary simply so you can be retained and paid.

EXPERT PROMOTIONAL AVENUES

When an attorney needs an expert witness for a case, most will have their staff search online. That is when you want your information to be visible and accessible. Online directories are the easiest way to achieve this. There will be multiple results from multiple directories, so the best approach to maximize your response and ensure that you are found is to list yourself in multiple directories. These directories may charge monthly or annual fees for their services. The fees may at first glance seem to be an added and unnecessary expense. However, if you simply land one case annually, you will more than likely recoup the cost of the listing. At the risk of promotion, a few more commonly used legal expert directories are listed here for your own perusing:

JurisPro
https://www.jurispro.com

SEAK
https://www.seakexperts.com/

Round Table Group

https://www.roundtablegroup.com/

Many more reputable expert directories will go beyond simply listing those who paid to be found through a search. They may offer specific types of expert training, perform credential verifications of experts, and many more amenities that will alleviate the work of an attorney in finding the best expert for one's case.

One simple consideration to take into account includes the words you use on a webpage and the services you acquire to promote key words that would appear in search engines. Different key words and phrases may appear in some search findings yet not others. The reason for this? It is simply based on what classification terms the directory opts to use to categorize their experts. For example, your specific expertise may be related to sudden cardiac death. However, an expert directory firm may not use such a subspecialty term and rather classify a group as "medicine" or "emergency care." In fact, your expertise within sudden cardiac death may yield cases stemming from youth athletic fields, yet there may not be any connection between how you promote yourself and the terms the directory uses when a lawyer or paralegal searches a specific term such as "sports medicine," "youth sports," or "sport safety." The way to maximize one's search engine capabilities is to ensure your profiles are inclusive of the key words and phrases and, if not, discuss the options with the directories to add. When using your own website, you may not have the greatest reach or popularity among lawyers searching for experts, but you do control 100% of the terms you use to promote your services.

Expert Promotional Pitfalls

Despite all of the wisdom one possesses as an expert, it counts for nothing in the absence of good common sense when it comes to promoting oneself. Part of learning how the medicolegal system works includes putting oneself out there as an expert in a way that does not backfire in terms of retaining cases and/or landing a case and having your own materials used against you. With that, more of the common promotional pitfalls are discussed.

- **Cheap Marketing Tactics.** Expert work should not be viewed as a hobby. Rather, it is a real business affecting the lives of real people. With that said, a professional who seeks expert work and intentionally promotes oneself should do so by viewing marketing and promotional expenses as an investment as opposed to an expense. Invest professionally, and a return on your investment is more likely to occur.

- *Generic Social Media Plan.* Social media platforms such as Facebook, Twitter, or other avenues can serve as helpful marketing approaches. However, simply saying you are using social media to market is a generic approach. What is your message? Are your followers the appropriate target audience? Are your messages resulting in leads for cases? What type of analytics do you use to measure your success? The bottom line—simply being active on social media takes time and may not be a good use of one's time without verification of the efforts leading to outcomes.

- *Abundance of Expertise.* An expert signifies by its very own definition that one is at the top of the knowledge pyramid in a single given area of content. While it is not uncommon for professionals in the health care industry to possess expertise in a few related areas, a promotion of too many areas of expertise may be seen as a red flag and a concern of overzealous marketing that could lead to no cases.

- *Embellishment.* Arguably one of the most dangerous paths to go down as an expert is to be cross-examined and have your credentials or accomplishments challenged in a way that is an exaggerated reflection of the true facts. Be sure to review, and review again, the wording and the factual descriptions used to convey titles, positions, and other achievements.

- *Improper Fees.* Establishing a fee structure has been discussed previously in this book. It is not always an easy thing to set. It may not be the best thing to put out for public knowledge when marketing yourself as an expert and instead best conveyed when requested. However, in some instances, including that of working with some directories, you must make your fees known upfront. Simply put, charging fees that are on the low side may convey a message of being "less than expert," and charging fees on the high side may turn off some third parties. With that said, higher fees in some cases may also send a signal of an experienced expert. Either way, be sure to be able to explain and justify all of your fees in a reasonable and professional manner.

- *No Fee Structure Plan.* Not having any planned-out fee structure is worse than a poor fee structure. Besides being ill-prepared to share, it signals to others a lack of experience.

- *Missed Target.* At the end of the day, whatever format or medium one uses to market and promote expert services should be designed to reach those who would do the retaining. No matter how professional the information is, if it does not reach the target audience, it will not yield expert case work.

Chapter 10

Dos and Don'ts of an Expert

Life is a tightrope walk. One has to balance the dos and don'ts.

—Haresh Sippy

Chapter Objectives

At the completion of this chapter, you will:

- Be knowledgeable of the best practices for an expert to follow
- Be knowledgeable of what types of errors to avoid as an expert

This final chapter is a simple overview of the most common dos and don'ts for an expert to adhere to. These apply to different phases of expert work, from marketing and promotion to expertise development to deposition and trial testimony. All in all, the list could be much longer. Most content experts are not remotely close to being experts in the legal system, and as the old adage goes, "They don't know what they don't know." As a result, basic mistakes are made and can be costly in many ways. Therefore, it is imperative to learn as much as you can as it pertains to the role of an expert. These are what we feel are the top 10.

Konin JG, Ramey MS. *Becoming an Expert Witness in Health Care and Litigation: A Beginner's Guide* (pp 75-79).

Dos and Don'ts

1. **Do** establish yourself as an expert.

    Don't claim to be an expert in too many areas.

    For the most part, the law states that you can be qualified as an expert if you have the necessary, appropriate, and relevant education, training, or experience. Possessing an accredited degree in the health care field is the minimum standard. Establishing oneself in a focused area of expertise by means of published manuscripts, original research, invited speaking engagements, and other methods is important. One should avoid being portrayed as a "self-proclaimed" expert and instead be able to point to other sources as verified recognition of one's expertise. Additionally, maintaining a focused area within a discipline or even across a discipline is important to stay abreast with contemporary expertise and not spread too thin in too many areas of proposed content. An expert who possesses outstanding speaking skills and the ability to articulate complex scenarios into easily understandable facts will be more successful.

2. **Do** provide expert services for plaintiffs and defendants.

    Don't shift too heavily toward one side.

    One of the very first questions an expert will be asked is what percentage of cases they have worked for the plaintiff and for the defendant. While experts typically never know where the next contact will come from, they can be perceived as a so-called hired gun when work is tilted toward working with either side for a majority of the times being retained. The professional opinion and testimony of a "hired gun" may be challenged since the hiring counsel will be accused of retaining the expert, knowing what side the expert is likely to take in advance. Good experts will honestly be able to articulate facts that could in effect benefit both sides in an honest manner.

3. **Do** be sure all promoted information is accurate.

    Don't falsify, exaggerate, or omit information.

    An expert's curriculum vitae (CV) serves as the qualifying document to comprehensively describe one's career experience. It serves to provide the foundation for one's expertise, and it lays out a timeline of a body of work that will be scrutinized by all parties, especially the opposing counsel. It is beyond crucial that this document is proofread multiples times, maintains currency, and is accurate absent any form of exaggeration. A strong CV can result in an uncontested declaration of one's role as an expert. This would minimize any time spent qualifying the expert, a process referred to as a "voir dire." To the contrary, a CV riddled with errors, omissions, and/or exaggerations will become the focus of one's line of questioning.

4. **Do** have an established verifiable fee structure and retainer agreement.

   Don't price your fees too low or too high or have a less-than-professional retainer agreement.

   Possessing a detailed and well-thought-out retainer agreement inclusive of one's fee schedule not only demonstrates one's level of expert experience but also serves to protect the expert by way of a binding legal contractual relationship with a retaining party. Clearly outlining as many of the services to be performed avoids unknown and uneasy discussions after the fact. While misunderstanding can occur, experience and good mentorship will provide an expert with the information needed to identify the terms within any retainer. One of the most common negotiable aspects of the retainer is one's fees. Such fees should also be carefully thought out before providing to counsel in an initial document. Both real and perceived concerns can be viewed and expressed with inappropriate pricing of one's fees for service.

5. **Do** be sure to carefully screen for conflicts of interest.

   Don't accept a case until you are certain you have screened for all potential conflicts.

   Disclosing any potential conflicts of interest should be done as soon as possible, possibly even before signing any retainer agreement. Conflicts may range from performing work previously for any of the parties to having a known relationship with anyone named in a case. In some cases, conflicts are not known immediately and should be reported once brought to an expert's attention. Conflicts that are disclosed do not always rule out an expert. However, if not disclosed and found later, they will almost certainly go against one's ability to provide expert opinion and testimony. In some cases, the retaining counsel may identify a potential concern related to a conflict that the expert is unaware of. This underlines the importance of the expert to share as much information as possible to the counsel as necessary to avoid the case taking a turn for the worse.

6. **Do** proofread all written reports.

   Don't submit a report in a rush without carefully reviewing.

   While experts are not perfect, they are expected to proofread carefully any written document that one attaches a name to. Attention to detail of the written word is essential and should include the obvious—correcting typos, word omissions, and improper punctuation and using proper grammar as much as possible. Additionally, the content of a report itself should be looked over as many times as possible to avoid omission of key facts, ensure accurate chronological events, and include evidence where necessary. When possible, use of a peer expert review comes in handy to verify an errorless report is submitted.

7.   **Do** enter a deposition prepared.

Don't enter a deposition overconfident or underprepared.

A deposition can be grueling and nerve-racking regardless of how many times one participates in the process. An expert is expected to be prepared and know the facts of the case as much as possible and compare the facts to one's expert knowledge. Preparation includes being in communication with one's retaining counsel and knowing all of the documents used for the basis of one's testimony. In addition, an expert's demeanor can also play a role in demonstrating a sense of comfort and confidence, yet not arrogance or overconfidence. Body language, eye contact, tone, resonance, and likability all play into the perception of one's credibility.

8.   **Do** stick to the evidence and facts of a case.

Don't try to answer quickly and recall based solely on memory.

When being asked questions by attorneys, one can have a tendency to feel the nerves kick in and the pressure to provide a relatively quick response. In fact, a factual response is best, regardless of the speed with which it is provided. An expert should never rely on memory recall simply to provide an answer. Rather, refer to documents when needed, and take your time prior to answering. If unable to recall, saying "I do not recall" is appropriate and best. Questions may be intentionally designed to catch an expert in a twist of facts, so always be sure of what answers are being conveyed.

9.   **Do** know your limits as an expert when retained.

Don't play the role of an attorney.

A good expert (and sometimes even a not-so-good expert) may feel a tendency to go beyond the expert role and cross the line of the responsibilities of a lawyer. Experts play a valuable role but do not possess the training and expertise or understand the "why" of what is behind the skill set of lawyering. There are times when an expert will be asked by an attorney to assist with developing cross-examination questions for an opposing expert, but this should never be interpreted or self-claimed as lawyering.

10. **Do** understand the task of transferring expert language to more simplistic terms.

Don't overly impress with language understood only by fellow experts.

A good expert, and a good story-teller for that matter, can relate a message to an audience of varying ages, educational levels, and background. Health care experts possess knowledge at a high level that oftentimes includes words not familiar to the general public. Breaking down medical terms, as well as explaining complicated medical maneuvers, interventions, and conditions in lay terms, is an expertise in and of itself. In a sense, it is much like speaking to colleagues at a grand rounds session in the morning and then pivoting to treating patients just minutes later. This is a skill set health care providers practice daily and typically become good at. This transcends into the role of an expert where you are called upon for your advanced knowledge and asked to translate it into lay terms.

GLOSSARY

affidavit: A written statement confirmed by oath and/or affirmation, for use as evidence in court.

compensation: The terms of an expert's financial retention or payment for testimony.

complete report: A statement of opinion written by an expert that must include all opinions that one intends to reference with court testimony.

conflict of interest: A situation in which the concerns or aims of two different parties are incompatible and/or a situation in which a person is in a position to derive personal benefit from actions or decisions made in their official capacity.

consulting expert: An expert who will never be asked to testify and only serves to provide consultation.

cross-examination: Inquiry made into each of the opinions that an expert renders with questions posed by the opposing counsel.

date of loss: An initiating traumatic event that is alleged to have legally caused the injury and resulting damages sought.

***Daubert* motion:** The court, or judge, will serve as a gatekeeper to ensure consistency and that any and all scientific testimony or evidence admitted is not only relevant but reliable.

defendant: The party in a lawsuit denying or defending the claim.

deposition: Process whereby an expert provides a sworn testimony.

direct examination: Inquiry made into each of the opinions that an expert renders with questions posed by the retaining counsel.

discovery: An inquiry of information by an attorney of an expert, including but not limited to background, education, training, experience, and basis of opinions.

engagement letter: A contractual written document between the expert and the retaining counsel that outlines the responsibilities of each party.

Federal Rule of Civil Procedure 26(a)(2)(A): Requires a party to disclose the identity of any potential trial witness who will give expert testimony.

Federal Rule of Civil Procedure 26(a)(2)(B): States a testifying expert must disclose all information that has been considered in forming one's opinion.

Federal Rule of Civil Procedure 26(a)(2)(C): Requires an expert's report due no later than 90 days prior to trial.

Federal Rule of Civil Procedure 26(b)(4)(B): States a consulting expert is not required to disclose information unless under "exceptional circumstances" that make it "impractical" to obtain information from any other way.

Konin JG, Ramey MS. *Becoming an Expert Witness in Health Care and Litigation: A Beginner's Guide* (pp 81-83). © 2023 SLACK Incorporated.

Federal Rule of Civil Procedure 30(b)(4): Provides for the taking of depositions by means other than traditional stenographic.

Federal Rule of Civil Procedure 56(e): Requires that affidavits "shall be made on personal knowledge and shall set forth such facts as would be admissible in evidence."

Federal Rule of Evidence 104(a): Provides that preliminary questions concerning the qualification of a person to be a witness, or the admissibility of evidence, shall be determined by the court.

Federal Rule of Evidence 403 (Exclusion): Authorizes the exclusion of any relevant testimony if its probative value is substantially outweighed by the danger of unfair prejudice, confusion of the issues, or misleading the jury.

Federal Rule of Evidence 701 (Lay Witness): A witness whose testimony in the form of opinions or inferences is limited to those opinions or inferences rationally based on perception and/or helpful to clear understanding.

Federal Rule of Evidence 702 (Expert Witness): A witness whose testimony is based on scientific, technical, or other specialized knowledge.

Federal Rule of Evidence 703: A requirement that experts base their testimony on reliable facts and data.

Federal Rule of Evidence 705: An expert can give an opinion without disclosing the underlying facts or data on which they relied in formulating that opinion, but a party must be careful not to include too little in the affidavit in light of the requirements of the Federal Rule of Civil Procedure 56(e).

fee structure: A representation of the various services that you will provide as an expert and the remuneration requested for each.

legal standard: A level by which an expert's opinion meets a reasonable degree of certainty as opposed to being likely or possible.

letter of protection: A form signed by the medical professional, patient, and legal counsel that promises to pay for medical care through proceeds of the litigation.

motion for summary judgment: A judgment that asks the court to issue a final decision on the qualifications and opinions of an expert.

peer review: A process whereby a primary expert may have been retained and a secondary expert is hired simply to review the primary expert's findings.

plaintiff: The party in a lawsuit bringing the claim.

preliminary opinion: A verbal or written opinion provided by the consulting expert to the client.

presuit analysis: Documentation of background materials to facilitate a substantive discussion upon which a retained expert will be directed to review and provide opinions.

qualifications: A comprehensive list of an expert's status to qualify in such a role, to include, but is not limited to, one's education, experience, and publication record.

replenishable retainer: A retainer whereby the expert deducts billable hours from the fees that have already been paid in the retainer.

retained: Term used to secure a contractual working agreement between a lawyer and an expert.

retainer fee: A form of a deposit provided to the expert in good faith as part of being retained and accepting the engagement terms.

spoliation of evidence: A process of which leads to evidence put forth by an expert is not preserved.

statement of all opinion: A written document outlining the reasons and underlying basis of an expert's professional opinion.

summary judgment: The court's ruling or final judgment on an expert's qualifications and opinion.

testifying (designated) expert: An expert who will provide sworn testimony via deposition or trial.

two-prong test: States that (1) the subject of an expert's testimony must be scientific knowledge and (2) must "assist" the trier of fact further characterized as "relevant to the task at hand" in that it "logically advances a material aspect of the proposing parties' case."

BIBLIOGRAPHY

Chapter 1

Fed. R. Evid. 104.

Fed. R. Evid. 403.

Fed. R. Evid. 701.

Fed. R. Evid. 702.

Fed. R. Evid. 703.

Chapter 2

Daubert v. Merrell Dow Pharmaceuticals, Inc., 509 U.S. 579 (1993).

Frye v. United States, 293 F. 1013 (D.C. Cir. 1923).

Chapter 4

Fed. R. Civ. P. 26(a)(2)(B).

Fed. R. Civ. P. 26(b)(4)(B).

Chapter 5

Fed. R. Civ. P. 26.

Harvey Bay and Through Harvey v. General Motors Corp., 873 F.2d 1343 (10th Cir. 1989).

Howell v. Maytag, 36 Fed. R. Serv. 3d 945 (M.D. Pa. 1996).

Spearman Industries, Inc. v. St. Paul Fire and Marine Ins. Co., 128 F. Supp 2d 1148 (N.D. Ill. 2001).

Konin JG, Ramey MS. *Becoming an Expert Witness in Health Care and Litigation: A Beginner's Guide* (pp 85-86).
© 2023 SLACK Incorporated.

Chapter 6
Fed. R. Civ. P. 26.

Fed. R. Civ. P. 30(b)(4).

Fed. R. Civ. P. 56(e).

Fed. R. Evid. 702.

Fed. R. Evid. 703.

Fed. R. Evid. 705.

Chapter 7
Eckstein M, Nyffeler P. The expert of my enemy is my expert: conflicts of interest amongst expert witnesses. *Litigation News*. 2012;Summer:1, 4-6.

Eri C. How to run a conflict check for expert witnesses? October 29, 2013. https://www. forensisgroup.com/how-to-run-a-conflict-check-for-expert-witnesses-2/

Firestone J. Best practices for avoiding expert witness disqualification. June 23, 2020. https://www.expertinstitute.com/resources/insights/best-practices-for-avoiding-expert-witness-disqualification/

Chapter 8
American Academy of Pediatrics. Guidelines for expert witness testimony in medical malpractice litigation. *Pediatrics*. 2002;109(5):974-979. https://pediatrics. aappublications.org/content/109/5/974. Accessed September 15, 2020.

Larson A. Sample contract for expert witness services. Expert Law. May 7, 2018. https://www.expertlaw.com/library/expert_witness/expert_contract_1.html. Accessed September 15, 2020.

Markowitz J. Creating a fee schedule for expert consultation and testimony. *Forensic Healthcare Online*. July 24, 2014. https://www.forensichealth.com/2014/07/24/creating-a-fee-schedule-for-expert-consultation-and-testimony/. Accessed September 15, 2020.

Chapter 9
American Marketing Association. Definitions of marketing. https://www.ama.org/the-definition-of-marketing-what-is-marketing/. Accessed September 26, 2020.

Martinez T. 13 easy marketing methods for the expert witness. https://blog. testifyingexpert.com/articles/2019/13-Easy-Marketing-Methods-for-the-Expert-Witness.php. Accessed September 26, 2020.

INDEX

CPSIA information can be obtained
at www.ICGtesting.com
Printed in the USA
JSHW060233160922
30581JS00004B/13